SECRETS SUSPECTS SEEDS & SOIL

KEN STEWART

K&D
PUBLISHING ·

DrKenStewart.com

Secrets, Suspects, Seeds & Soil

ISBN 978-1-09837-958-2
ISBN 978-1-09837-959-9
Copyright © 2021 by Kennith E. Stewart, D.Min.

Published by K & D Publishing, LLC
P. O. Box 470511
Tulsa, Oklahoma 74147

Unless otherwise noted all Scriptures in this book are taken from the KING JAMES VERSION (KJV): KING JAMES VERSION, public domain.

Scriptures marked CJB are taken from the COMPLETE JEWISH BIBLE (CJB): Scripture taken from the COMPLETE JEWISH BIBLE, copyright© 1998 by David H. Stern. Published by Jewish New Testament Publications, Inc. www.messianicjewish. net/ jntp. Distributed by Messianic Jewish Resources Int'l. www.messianicjewish.net. All rights reserved. Used by permission.

Scriptures marked ERV are taken from the HOLY BIBLE: EASY-TO-READ VERSION © 2001 by World Bible Translation Center, Inc. and used by permission.

Scriptures marked ESV are taken from the THE HOLY BIBLE, ENGLISH STANDARD VERSION (ESV): Scriptures taken from THE HOLY BIBLE, ENGLISH STANDARD VERSION * Copyright© 2001 by Crossway, a publishing ministry of Good News Publishers. Used by permission.

Scriptures marked HCSB are taken from the HOLMAN CHRISTIAN STANDARD BIBLE (HCSB): Scripture taken from the HOLMAN CHRISTIAN STANDARD BIBLE, copyright© 1999, 2000, 2002, 2003 by Holman Bible Publishers, Nashville Tennessee. All rights reserved.

Scripture marked KJ21 are taken from The Holy Bible, 21st Century King James Version (KJ21®), Copyright © 1994, Deuel Enterprises, Inc., Gary, SD 57237, and used by permission.

Scriptures marked NIV are taken from THE HOLY BIBLE, NEW INTERNATIONAL VERSION *. Copyright© 1973, 1978, 1984, 2011 by Biblica, Inc.™. Used by permission of Zondervan. All rights reserved worldwide.

Scriptures marked NKJV are taken from the NEW KING JAMES VERSION (NKJV): Scripture taken from the NEW KING JAMES VERSION®. Copyright© 1982 by Thomas Nelson, Inc. Used by permission. All rights reserved.

Contents

Acknowledgments

———

Donna Stewart - Thank you for over 50 years of life with you by my side as my precious wife. Your love and full support have always meant more to me than I have words to express. You have often referred to yourself as my number one fan. I know this to be true. Your actions and your words have proven it. Because of you I have been able to devote my life to learning the kind of material I have shared on these pages. Any reward I may seem to deserve actually belongs to you.

Jason Stewart - Thank you for lending your God-given talent in the design of the artwork for this book. It will always serve as an example of what is possible when a person places their full confidence in God and is willing to pursue their own dream. I love working with you and having your advise and input in what I do for God.

Introduction

For years I have observed the spiritual battles of many Christians. Often, I have wondered if there might be one specific concept to be found in the Word of God which would benefit all of these individuals. I was not looking for a magic solution or cure all. My desire was to discover a common place to which I could direct people which would help them go on to embrace the changes needed in their lives. This desire reflects my understanding of God's Word and our relationship to it. The Bible is the book by which we must live our lives.

In a world void of absolutes, filled with people doing what is right in their own eyes, I see the Word of God as the standard by which all of us are measured. This is true even when we don't want to agree with what it says. Many Christians view the Bible in the same way. The problem is found, in not knowing what to do about this.

One day as I was making preparation to teach, I was motivated by the Spirit of God to take a fresh look at what is known as the **Parable of the Sower.** This parable has often been used to teach things about giving money to the church. I have never used it in this way. I am not saying this is an incorrect use of this passage of Scripture. It has just never been my approach to this passage.

The more I studied this parable and the explanation Jesus gave of it the more I realized Jesus was expressing something much more profound than I had ever heard. Jesus was not just teaching on seeds or soil. Jesus was teaching on the subject of understanding; especially understanding the Kingdom of Heaven. I knew this was an important key to understanding The Kingdom of God.

Some will read this and they will say, of course Jesus was teaching on understanding. It says this right in the Scripture. In verse 13 Jesus made this statement regarding the crowd that day: *"neither do they understand."*

In Matthew 13:15 I discovered the answer I had searched for all these years. It is hidden in plain sight in these words of Jesus.

> *Lest at any time they should see with their eyes and hear with their ears, and should understand with their heart, and should be converted, and I should heal them.*

At first my attention was drawn to the fact Jesus seemed to be expressing a reason not to see these people converted or healed. I thought surely this can't be what a loving, caring Jesus means by these words. It was then the Spirit of God revealed to me what was intended.

Three very important steps are necessary for salvation. The Apostle Paul said:

> *That if thou shalt confess with thy mouth the Lord Jesus, and shalt believe in thine heart that God hath raised him from the dead, thou shalt be saved. (Romans 10:9)*

However, Jesus made this much clearer when He said: People must *see with their eyes.* This means they must see the truth and see the lies they have been drawn to in the past. We have prayed many times for the eyes of the unsaved to be opened to the truth. This is step one.

Then they must *hear with their ears.* We have done an excellent job with this part of the plan. Hundreds of thousands of hours; perhaps millions of hours have been spent these past 2000 years proclaiming the Gospel that Jesus saves. This is step two.

It is the third step, where I believe we have been very weak. Jesus said *they should understand with their heart.* This is the topic of this book.

At this point of discovery, my mind was flooded with questions. What does it mean to understand with the heart? How do we help people understand with the heart? What is it their hearts need to understand? What is it my heart has understood for over 70 years so many others do not seem to understand? Why don't they understand with their heart? What is the solution?

I noticed Jesus had included healing in these statements. Now those words had new meaning. I realized why it can be so difficult to get some people healed. It is a matter of the heart. I don't mean sin or un-forgiveness in their heart. These things **can be** what blocks healing. But I am talking about not having an understanding heart.

What is an understanding heart and how do we get one? I intend to answer this question in the following pages. This is my task in this book. I intend to explain what an understanding heart is. By the time I finish this discourse, my goal is to make it very clear how to develop an understanding heart. I want to motivate you more than ever to have such a heart.

I have found the proper ingredients to do this. It is contained in this thirteenth chapter of Matthew's Gospel. Jesus spoke about the Word of the Kingdom. When He used this phrase, He was talking about the Word of God. I will be using these two phrases interchangeably to help you grasp the depth of their meaning.

We are a part of something very special. It is the Kingdom of Heaven. It is made up entirely of people who have been converted. The people in this kingdom are intended to live out their time on this earth in good health. We are to do this by participating in The Kingdom of God.

Is it possible these Kingdoms have their own language?

Then said Jesus unto them, When ye have lifted up the Son of man, then shall ye know that I am he, and that I do nothing of myself; but as my Father hath taught me, I speak these things. (John 8:28)

In the Kingdom of God, should we be speaking the words we find in the Bible? This is where we find the words of our Father. How different our lives would be if we only spoke those things our Heavenly Father has taught us. I am quite sure this is the way things are done in Heaven. Start thinking about doing the same on earth.

Here is another very important phrase Jesus used in this parable.

He answered and said unto them, because it is given unto you to know the mysteries of the Kingdom of Heaven, but to them it is not given. (Matthew 13:11)

There are two intriguing phrases in this statement. Jesus mentioned the Kingdom of Heaven. Then He also spoke of the mysteries of this kingdom.

Connect these things together in your mind. The words spoken in Heaven are all from one source. This source is the Father. In Heaven we will only say the things the Father has taught us. Jesus did this while He was here on this earth. Jesus also told us we are at this very moment a part of the Kingdom of Heaven. As we are actively involved in the Kingdom of God on this earth, why shouldn't we be talking like they do in Heaven? These two Kingdoms are tightly connected. How many people really understand this? This is one of the mysteries of the Kingdom of Heaven.

I will have much to say about the mysteries of the Kingdom of Heaven. There are many of them. I will tell you what some of them are in the pages which follow. This is the pathway to developing an understanding heart. Perhaps I should state it in this manner.

When you understand just one small thing about the Kingdom of Heaven you have begun the process of developing an understanding heart. However, the proof you have understood, is when this one small thing becomes a vital part of you. It becomes something you do without needing to think about it first. You are more Kingdom of Heaven minded. You think, speak and act like a citizen of Heaven. You are still very much on this earth, but you act more like you are in Heaven. We call this The Kingdom of God. As you embrace each mystery I share with you and as you discover other mysteries on your own, your understanding heart will increase.

I trust you enjoy what I have discovered!

Chapter One

With All Thy Getting Get Understanding

———

In my world view, deception and understanding are opposites. **Deception** is a deliberate attempt to create a **misunderstanding**. The intent is to cause a person to think something and/or to do something which they should not think or do.

Creating **understanding** is a deliberate attempt to bring reason and **common sense** to a person so they will think and do as they should.

When I was very young, I discovered if I really understood something, I could use it. Perhaps everybody knows this, but until I made this discovery on my own, I did not know how important understanding really is.

I ask a lot of questions; and it is much more than a thirst for knowledge; or just being curious. I have a great desire to understand the ways of God better than I have ever understood them. You could sum up my life as a quest for understanding. This is the reason for all of the questions I ask that start with the word **why**.

For example: I am very happy about all the reports of people being healed of various diseases in our church services. However, I want to understand why we are not seeing even more people receive their healing. Believe me when I say I know all of the typical reasons which have been given.

One of the most common reasons given for sick people not being healed is that they have sin in their lives. This sounds too Biblical to just let it pass.

> *And as Jesus passed by, he saw a man which was blind from his birth. And his disciples asked him, saying, Master, who did sin, this man, or his parents, that he was born blind? Jesus answered, Neither hath this man sinned, nor his parents: but that the works of God should be made manifest in him. I must work the works of him that sent me, while it is day: the night cometh, when no man can work. As long as I am in the world, I am the light of the world. (John 9:1-5)*

The disciples were of the opinion when a terrible

thing happens, such as a child being born blind, sin must have been involved. Yet, the answer given by Jesus is very clear. "*Neither hath this man sinned, nor his parents.*" How wonderful it would be if the text stopped with those words. We would have a clear understanding regarding the matter of sickness and disease and birth defects. It would be easy to say they are not necessarily caused by sin. Frankly, this is exactly the position I take on the issue.

The challenge is what the translators chose to do with the few words which follow the statement about neither the blind man nor his parents having sin in their lives.

> *But that the works of God should be made manifest in him.*

The **structure** of the verses causes this statement by Jesus to sound as though this man was born blind to bring glory to God. Some have said that having a blind man conveniently available gave Jesus a chance to do the works of God. **I do not agree** with this conclusion. My understanding of the rest of Scripture convinces me there is a problem with the manner in which these sentences have been framed.

I find no evidence in the Word of God for the Devil doing things to help God out in manifesting what God can do. In fact, Jesus made clear the difference in what the thief is here to do and what Jesus came to do.

The thief cometh not, but for to steal, and to kill, and to destroy: I am come that they might have life, and that they might have it more abundantly. (John 10:10)

These statements convince me there is a problem with the common translation of what Jesus said in response to the question asked by His disciples. I will restate what Jesus said by making three minor changes to the punctuation of these sentences. The response from Jesus should read as follows.

And His disciples asked Him, saying, Master, who did sin, this man, or his parents, that he was born blind? Jesus answered, neither hath this man sinned, nor his parents. But that the works of God should be made manifest in him; I must work the works of him that sent me, while it is day. The night cometh, when no man can work.

Some would argue what I have done is dangerous. I believe the translators made a mistake. To be correct, translation of scripture, depends as much on consistent and coherent theology, as it does on the choice of the meaning of any Hebrew or Greek word. I have done enough translation work to know how important choosing the correct meaning of words can be. Translation is at its best when these elements are properly combined.

The judgment of the accuracy of all translations of Scripture must be based on rightly dividing the Word of truth. **Rightly dividing the Word of truth has nothing to do with my opinion.** It has everything to do with what can be determined about any topic by looking at all of the other Scriptures which can be found on the same topic. I only gave you one example in this discussion. There are many more to back up my claim the Devil is not in the business of helping God and neither does God assist the Devil in achieving his goals.

It is my firm contention these types of mistakes in translation have added to the confusion many people have about God's will to make them well. Some have even declared publicly they are willing to suffer so the works of God could be made manifest (someday) in them. How very sad. Yet, they do not understand!

It is my desire to understand why it is easy to get some people healed and hard to get other people healed. I also want to understand why some diseases seem to respond to the healing anointing more readily than others.

Jesus certainly did not have these issues. Why do we have them?

In our ministry, blind eyes are being opened and cancer is being healed. At the same time, people still have high blood pressure and diabetes and others need joint replacements and cataract surgery. I want to understand why. Frankly, to my natural mind this does not make sense.

I am not finding fault in any manner. I know all of the reasons we have been given by some awesome men and women of God in the past. I have a deep appreciation for the understanding I have received from them.

But I must ask, "what do we still not understand?"

I can't ignore these statements in scripture regarding the healing ministry of the Lord Jesus.

> *But when Jesus knew it, He withdrew Himself from thence: and great multitudes followed Him, and He healed them all; (Matthew 12:15)*

> *Now when the sun was setting, all they that had any sick with divers diseases brought them unto Him; and He laid his hands on every one of them, and healed them. (Luke 4:40)*

> *And the whole multitude sought to touch Him: for there went virtue out of Him, and healed them all. (Luke 6:19)*

Yes - this was Jesus and I am not Jesus.

But this same Jesus said: *"verily, verily, I say unto you, he that believeth on me, the works that I do shall he do also; and greater works than these shall he do; because I go unto my father."* (John 14:12)

I expect to be able to do the same things Jesus did!

As brazen as this statement may sound, it is still my desire to see every sick person healed. Otherwise, I see no way to ever do greater works than Jesus did. It is rare to find another person who really believes this is possible. It is harder to find one willing to declare we should take these statements by Jesus to be literal. I find myself once again asking why this is the case.

Why is it so hard to imagine doing the same things Jesus did? I will answer this question with one statement.

We do not have the understanding we need.

My simple statement can be broken down into two parts. First, we do not really understand how Jesus did many of the things we read about in the Bible. Secondly, we do not understand why we fail to do even the smallest of things which Jesus did on a daily basis.

It is truly an honor to be used by God to bring healing and the miraculous into so many lives. Just so it stays clear in the mind of every person who reads these pages I want to state emphatically; **I take no credit** for any good thing God has done. But I do expect it to continue.

I have decided not to accept the answers we have been given or the answers we have been using, without searching the Word and asking God to show me more. Too many people need healing to accept the status quo without question.

Doubt and unbelief, and people not growing in faith is a problem. I do understand this. But what about those of us in ministry; are we doing our part? Are we doing what God expects of us? What was it men and women like John G. Lake and Kathryn Kuhlman knew; that we should know?

If Jesus walked the earth today would He say we know all we need to know about miracles and healing? I don't think so. In fact, **I know He would not!**

What more do we need to understand so this great move of God never stops until Jesus returns? This has been prophesied many times. Are we ready?

Often, I think about the great healing revivals. I think about the many wonderful people of God I have had the privilege of knowing. Then I think about how they did all they knew to do, to bring us to this point in time.

I can only conclude, for years God has been planning something truly wonderful. Our Heavenly Father has been carefully preparing us for this day. **It is our turn to see the great works of our awesome God.**

According to what we find in the Word of God we are more than well equipped to do the task assigned to us by the Lord Jesus. I am thinking of some of the statements He made such as this one.

> *It is the Spirit that quickeneth; the flesh profiteth nothing: the words that I speak unto you, they are Spirit, and they are life. (John 6:63)*

I also recall these powerful words from the prophet Isaiah.

> *So shall My word be that goeth forth out of My mouth: it shall not return unto Me void, but it shall accomplish that which I please, and it shall prosper in the thing whereunto I sent it. (Isaiah 55:11)*

The quickening Spirit is here. He has been here since the day of Pentecost. The words Jesus spoke are **alive**. Both of these were given to us to bring life and health and healing. I find this same thinking expressed by the writer of the book of Proverbs.

My son, attend to my words; incline thine ear unto my sayings. Let them not depart from thine eyes; keep them in the midst of thine heart. For they are life unto those that find them, and health to all their flesh. Keep thy heart with all diligence; for out of it are the issues of life. (Proverbs 4:20-23)

I have reached the following conclusions. The idea great things God has done in the past were only sovereign acts of God is totally wrong. When I refer to these things as sovereign acts, I am talking about the notion God did things when and where He was ready. No one saw it coming. Most importantly, sovereignty of God, means no human had any responsibility for what took place.

This idea is totally **inconsistent** with the book of Acts. Consider what happened on the day of Pentecost. Jesus told the people to go to the upper room. Jesus told them to wait until the day of Pentecost. Jesus had talked to them about speaking with new tongues. This was well planned and revealed to the people who were involved. But the people had to do their part.

The same things can be said about what happened in Cornelius' house. God planned these events and revealed them to Peter while he was still at his home. All of this is recorded in the book of Acts. It is all there for us to read. But the people had to do their part.

Every time there has been a great move of God, much earnest **prayer has preceded it.**

What happened in The Azusa Street Revival in California a little over 100 years ago was preceded by a lot of prayer. Today, many people have been praying and prophesying and looking for God to do mighty things in this earth. This tells me we should be doing everything we can to prepare for what is surely headed our way. This is why I keep talking about the coming Great Awakening.

I have heard it said we should not try to understand healing, miracles, signs and wonders and the moving of the Spirit. We should appreciate these things but never seek to understand them. **Why not?**

If we are not supposed to understand these things, how are we supposed to do greater things than Jesus did? Jesus certainly seemed to know what He was doing and how to do it over and over again in every place He went.

If we are not supposed to understand these things why did God tell us to get understanding? Are we to assume He only meant for us to have understanding in the natural world and not in the realm of the Spirit?

Hear, ye children, the instruction of a father, and attend to know understanding. For I give you good doctrine, forsake ye not my law. For

I was my father's son, tender and only beloved in the sight of my mother. He taught me also, and said unto me, Let thine heart retain my words: keep my commandments, and live. Get wisdom, get understanding: forget it not; neither decline from the words of my mouth. Forsake her not, and she shall preserve thee: love her, and she shall keep thee. Wisdom is the principal thing; therefore get wisdom: and with all thy getting get understanding. (Proverbs 4:1-7)

Perhaps these Scriptures are a double reference in which the writer is speaking of his own words to a natural son. But these words can also be thought of as words spoken by our Father God to his sons. This proverb can correctly be viewed as a reference to the words which came from the mouth of God. Therefore, I believe these Scriptures give us a major clue to the way God wants to work in our lives.

Wisdom is usually the subject, when these verses are read and taught. And wisdom is very important. But the real emphasis is on **understanding**.

Get wisdom: and with all thy getting, get understanding.

Chapter Two

Three Very Important Words

———

As I contemplated the content of this chapter there were three words which stood out to me. These three words are **knowledge, wisdom** and **understanding**. Solomon used these words in Proverbs chapter 4. However, he never explained these words. Yet they are very important in the development of an understanding heart. I am talking about more than the use of the words. It is **the very distinct difference** in the meaning of the words which will be helpful to us. We will take a few minutes to look at them. I will also illustrate for you the reason I believe they are so important.

To help clarify the significance of these three words I will describe them in terms of the way they function most of the time. **Functionality** is the real issue.

Knowledge has to do with **facts**.

An easy way to think about this is to consider knowledge as having to do mostly with addressing **what** has happened. Or it could be **what is known** in a given situation. Of course, knowledge is also comprised of who is involved and perhaps when things occurred. To simplify matters we will only concern ourselves with the issue of **facts** which deal with **what**, to distinguish this word from the other two words.

Wisdom has more to do with **how** things happen. Wisdom is often thought of as the **skill** necessary to say or to do the right thing in the right way. Consider this.

In dealing with a particular matter I may know **what** needs to be said or done. I have the **facts**. However, I can create real problems with only the facts. If I do not have the **wisdom** necessary to say and do the right things I can cause chaos. My **lack of skill** can greatly outweigh my **knowledge of the facts** resulting in a terrible outcome.

Understanding encompasses the reason behind the things which happen in our lives. It is understanding which helps us to grasp the great and often mysterious **why** things occur. We have all been troubled and baffled because we did not understand why things happened. Why did a person die so young? Why did a person we wanted to be close to, not like us? Why was a terrible crime committed? Why doesn't God wipe out all the evil in the earth?

We may have the knowledge and may have a very good grasp of the **facts**. The details may be precisely known. With considerable **wisdom** we may have shared with others our opinions. Our **skill** helped them survive a horrible tragedy. Many years of ministry have placed me in such a position on numerous occasions. The most difficult challenge of all is explaining **why**. So many times, we are unable to express the reason. We simply do not have this depth of understanding.

I find the Hebrew meaning for each of these three words to be very helpful.

The Hebrew word for **know**[1] in Proverbs 4:1 means to acquire knowledge or to perceive. There are many ways to gather this knowledge. It is an accumulation of facts and other types of information, such as impressions.

The Hebrew word for **wisdom**[2] used in these Scriptures is defined as skill and shrewdness. We can accurately say wisdom has much to do with how to use knowledge.

The Hebrew word for **understanding**[3] means discernment. From this definition of the Hebrew word for understanding I concluded understanding helps us to grasp why things happen. The right understanding can explain the reason things happen the way they do. This understanding can also help us when we must explain difficult things to other people.

I would also surmise from the Hebrew meaning of the word understanding it includes discerning when and how to use this skill regarding the knowledge I have acquired.

These three words are often used in such an intertwined manner in the English language one could get the impression they can be used interchangeably. This is not correct. It creates confusion.

I will now take the meaning I have assigned to these three words and use a well-known story from the book of Acts to enhance our understanding.

The story begins in Acts chapter 3 when Peter and John healed a lame man at the Beautiful Gate of the Temple. It is hard for us to grasp; but these men were arrested for what they had done. We will pick up the story in chapter 4 of the book of Acts where we find these words.

> *Now when they saw the boldness of Peter and John, and perceived that they were unlearned and ignorant men, they marveled; and they took knowledge of them, that they had been with Jesus. (Acts 4:13)*

The religious people knew Jesus performed miracles. They had this much knowledge about Jesus. They also knew Peter and John had brought healing (a miracle) to this lame man. They had this much knowledge about them.

These religious leaders knew Peter and John had been with Jesus for several years. They had this knowledge. But **knowledge** is all they had. Knowledge alone is not enough.

These religious people knew **what** had happened. They did not know **how** it happened. And they did not seem to grasp **why**. There was a root cause for this **lack of understanding** in what had happened to the lame man. It is the fact they had absolutely **no understanding of what Jesus had done** in his death and resurrection. Their hearts were so hardened they did not understand why Jesus would care for a person this much. They had **knowledge** but were completely void of understanding.

The religious people had the **what** about the lame man. He was lame. He had never been able to walk. The man was born with this infirmity. But after the actions of Peter and John he could now walk. They were well informed of the facts. But they did not even care to know **how** this great miracle occurred. It had changed this man's life and they did not care!

The religious leaders did not know how Jesus did the wonderful things He accomplished in His ministry. They even went so far as to accuse Him of using demonic power. This tells us how void of understanding they really were. I am amazed every time I think about the attitude of these religious leaders. It defies common sense.

They did not know how Peter and John were able to perform this miracle. They did not want to know. Common sense would seem to dictate a basic level of curiosity. However, their minds were so blinded to the truth they could not bring themselves to ask the basic questions most humans would ask. Envy and hatred tend to make people blind.

More importantly they had no grasp and no interest in **why** this was possible. They did not care why this happened to the lame man. Such a huge void of compassion and caring for a man who had suffered so much is difficult to grasp. It simply reveals to us how much the Devil had infiltrated their thinking.

They were completely void of understanding!

At one of my meetings in the state of Alabama a young lady from Russia got in the prayer line one night when I was praying for the sick. I took her by the hands and she immediately fell to the floor when I touched her. She got up and I took her hands in mine once again. Down she went and fell on the floor again.

I asked her if she was born-again. The young lady said no. I touched her hands again and once more she fell on the floor. There was no struggle or violent action from her. There was no indication of demonic activity. She could not stand when the anointing of God touched her body.

I asked the girl if she would like to be born-again and she said no. Once more I took her by the hands and once again, she fell to the floor. This happened to her five different times.

The young lady did not understand what was happening to her or why it was happening. Much to my surprise she never asked me to explain. I am describing to you an event which took about 10 minutes. She never asked a single question.

The Spirit of God was really touching this young lady. Her eyes were big and wide. She had no idea what was going on. I gave her clear and easy to understand instructions regarding what she needed to do to receive Jesus as her Lord and Savior. I told her how to be saved. I taught her wisdom. But she refused to act on what I had shared with her.

I am convinced the young lady's refusal to act was not due to a lack of understanding. I made the **why** aspect of my discussion with her very clear. I even went so far as to tell her in front of the entire Church she was on her way to Hell if she did not give her heart to Jesus. She still refused.

At this point in the encounter I did not understand her lack of desire to give her heart to the Lord. The service ended and a lady, who knew the girl very well came and spoke to me. She told me what this girl's parents had said to her before she came to the United States. Her parents told her to never come back home to Russia if she became a Christian. **Now I understood why** she would not pray the sinner's prayer. The young lady was struggling with something I knew nothing about. It is often true an unknown factor is causing people to not act on what they do understand. By unknown factor, I am making reference to something we do not know as we observe their actions. This compels us to always speak and act with compassion.

Two weeks after my meeting in Alabama had ended and just before she flew home to Russia, this young lady prayed with the woman who had spoken to me, about her. She gave her heart to Jesus. I really wish I knew the rest of the story. I sincerely hope her parents saw enough change in her that they too became believers. I do expect to meet this young lady in Heaven.

Chapter Three

Understanding Has Two Sides

———

There are two very different sides to this matter of understanding. In order to explain what I mean by this statement we will look at some statements in Matthew chapter 13. When this parable is spoken of in sermons, this chapter of the Bible is often used to teach on the subject of **sowing seed**. This may be sowing the Word, or money, or good deeds. It is about much more.

After Jesus told the parable to His disciples, they asked Jesus why He was speaking to them in parables. The answer Jesus gave them is very enlightening.

> *And the disciples came, and said unto him, Why speakest thou unto them in parables? He answered and said unto them, Because it is given unto you to know the mysteries of the Kingdom of Heaven, but to them it is not given.*

For whosoever hath, to him shall be given, and he shall have more abundance: but whosoever hath not, from him shall be taken away even that he hath. Therefore speak I to them in parables: because they seeing see not; and hearing they hear not, neither do they understand. And in them is fulfilled the prophecy of Esaias, which saith, By hearing ye shall hear, and shall not understand; and seeing ye shall see, and shall not perceive: For this people's heart is waxed gross, and their ears are dull of hearing, and their eyes they have closed; lest at any time they should see with their eyes and hear with their ears, and should understand with their heart, and should be converted, and I should heal them. (Matthew 13:10-15)

Jesus told the disciples He **did not want the unbelievers** who were listening to **understand** what He was teaching. I know this sounds shocking. But this is what Jesus said to them. Jesus had a very good reason for His decision. His desire for them to not understand is something many Christians fail to grasp. Jesus was sharing with His disciples what He referred to as the mysteries of the Kingdom of Heaven. Out of compassion for the unbelievers, Jesus did not want them to be held responsible for things they would not participate in, either in this life or in the world to come. It should be clear, yes, Jesus was keeping **secrets**. He had a very good reason!

One of the problems we have had with these statements by Jesus is not really grasping we are a part of a very real kingdom. We are citizens of Heaven, even though we still live on this earth.

> *But our citizenship is in heaven. And we eagerly await a Savior from there, the Lord Jesus Christ, who, by the power that enables him to bring everything under his control, will transform our lowly bodies so that they will be like his glorious body. (Philippians 3:20-21 - NIV)*

Every kingdom has its own secrets. Every nation has its own secrets. There are many things about each country of the world which are only fully understood by the citizens of that nation. This is the way things work in the Kingdom of Heaven. If you want to know the **mysteries** of the Kingdom of Heaven, then become a citizen.

Why would Jesus tell the **secrets** of this great kingdom to people who had no desire nor interest in being a part of the kingdom? He would not do this and He did not do it. This is why He did not want them to understand what He was teaching.

Everything in your life you do not understand is a mystery. Think of it in this way. Because, once you understand, it is no longer a mystery. When something is no longer a mystery you may be able to benefit from it. Of course this depends on what the mystery was. You may choose to not act on what you understand.

The Bible tells us the Jewish people rejected Jesus.

> *He came unto his own, and his own received him not. But as many as received him, to them gave he power to become the sons of God, even to them that believe on his name: Which were born, not of blood, nor of the will of the flesh, nor of the will of man, but of God. And the Word was made flesh, and dwelt among us, (and we beheld his glory, the glory as of the only begotten of the Father,) full of grace and truth. (John 1:11-14)*

Since the Jewish people as a whole (during Jesus time on the earth) chose to reject Jesus, there was no possibility of them benefiting from the Kingdom of Heaven. **They were not citizens in this kingdom.** If they understood the mysteries (secrets) but could not benefit this would be remarkably cruel and unfair. So, even in their rejection of Jesus He still demonstrated great compassion for them.

As I have already shared with you, there is only one way into the kingdom. However, at this particular moment in his teaching, Jesus was not explaining the way to become a part of the Kingdom of Heaven. He was explaining some of its **secrets.** It was not beneficial for those who did not believe to understand these mysteries.

We can take this several steps further. One way the Devil blocks us from benefiting from the Kingdom of Heaven is by convincing those of us who do believe, that we can't understand the mysteries of the kingdom. He will even go so far as to try to convince us we should not try to understand. The Devil knows once we understand the mysteries of the kingdom, we can benefit from them. They are no longer special secrets only known by a few select people.

Here is the part of this passage in Matthew chapter 13 which struck me very forcibly. This is what led to the writing of this book. It was this statement in verse 15 of this chapter; *and should understand with their heart, and should be converted, and I should heal them.*

Jesus was describing the power of an understanding heart. This is a power not readily grasped by the body of Christ. In fact, I do believe it has often been confused with an understanding mind. These are two very different things.

When we are told in the Word not to lean on **our own understanding,** this is talking about our **mind** and **not our heart.** There is a major difference which I hope to make clear in the following pages.

Chapter Four

The Power of an Understanding Heart

———

There is a connection between understanding and salvation. When we explain the plan of salvation to most people they desire to be saved. Most of the time they will get saved once they understand. Fear, condemnation, and belittling sinners does not produce good results. Giving them **understanding** in their hearts **leads to salvation**. No doubt this is the reason, a very simple salvation message is always the best kind. This is also true of repentance. Romans 2:4 tells us: ...*the goodness of God leads you to repentance.* This certainly implies understanding.

Jesus connected healing to the understanding heart. This is in opposition to the things I have heard in my past. I have been told we could never understand healing. Perhaps we will never really understand exactly the **process** of how God's power heals people. But we can and we should understand it is His will and plan to heal us.

A lack of understanding kept the people spoken of in Matthew 13 from being healed. We know this is true because Jesus said so. This tells us **understanding is the path we should follow to be healed.**

I will explain why Jesus did not want to heal these people. Just making such a statement seems very radical. I am only following through on what Jesus said. Here is the explanation in another story in the Bible.

> *And, behold, a woman of Canaan came out of the same coasts, and cried unto him, saying, Have mercy on me, O Lord, thou son of David; my daughter is grievously vexed with a devil. But he answered her not a word. And his disciples came and besought him, saying, Send her away; for she crieth after us. But he answered and said, I am not sent but unto the lost sheep of the house of Israel. Then came she and worshiped him, saying, Lord, help me. But he answered and said, It is not meet to take the children's bread, and to cast it to dogs. And she said, Truth, Lord: yet the dogs eat of the crumbs which fall from their masters' table. Then Jesus answered and said unto her, O woman, great is thy faith: be it unto thee even as thou wilt. And her daughter was made whole from that very hour. (Matthew 15:22-28)*

I have thought much about this story. It has occurred to me, once again He was teaching His disciples a vital lesson. When Jesus made the comment about dogs, He was expressing how His disciples felt about this woman of Canaan. The disciples were **highly suspicious** of any person who was not one of them. When Jesus healed this woman's daughter, He let the whole world know how He felt about this woman and her daughter. His attitude varied greatly from theirs. In the process Jesus shared an exciting secret about the kingdom.

This **secret** is a tremendous truth about healing. Jesus called healing *"the children's bread."* We are the children of God. Jesus has made it clear healing belongs to God's children. **So, healing belongs to us!**

This woman of Canaan was not a Jew. She was not considered one of the children of God by her natural birth. Yet, when Jesus saw great faith in her he embraced her as one of the children of God. He then made this bread available to her. Her daughter was healed. Because of our faith in God we are now the children of God and this bread belongs to us. This is one of the blessings spoken of in the following Scriptures.

> *For ye are all the children of God by faith in Christ Jesus. For as many of you as have been baptized into Christ have put on Christ. There is neither Jew nor Greek, there is neither bond*

nor free, there is neither male nor female: for ye are all one in Christ Jesus. And if ye be Christ's, then are ye Abraham's seed, and heirs according to the promise. (Galatians 3:26-29)

A major key to getting people healed is increasing their level of understanding. Since I made a distinction between the understanding of the mind and the understanding heart I will add this further clarification.

Only the Word of God can bring understanding to the **heart**. Stories and testimonies appeal to the **senses**. They do reach the **mind** of the sick person and they are very important. But remember it is **only the Word of God that can divide between the soul and the spirit** of man. We must bring people who are sick to that place of understanding the Word so this understanding has an impact on their **heart**.

If you have been inclined to question that the promises of God belong to you; I have a message for you. This is no different to thinking you are somehow outside of the kingdom. I encourage you to stop seeing yourself in a negative way. If you are born-again, then you are one of God's children. You belong in the Kingdom of Heaven. **The mysteries are yours to understand.**

Chapter Five

Secrets Revealed and Suspects Identified

———

Matthew chapter 13 is well known for being a chapter comprised of numerous parables. In fact, these verses are descriptive of the entire chapter.

> *All these things spake Jesus unto the multitude in parables; and without a parable spake he not unto them: That it might be fulfilled which was spoken by the prophet, saying, I will open my mouth in parables; I will utter things which have been kept secret from the foundation of the world. (Matthew 13:34-35)*

By teaching the multitudes using parables Jesus accomplished several things. He was teaching those who believed in Him several key things about the Kingdom of Heaven. He was fulfilling a prophecy. He was revealing things which had been kept **secret** from the foundation of the world. He was keeping these things **secret** from people who refused to believe in Him. They still are secret to this day to the people who do not believe in Him as their Lord.

The reason many of the things prophesied about Jesus came to pass was because **He acted on them.** If something is prophesied to us, we must determine if we believe it is accurate. If so, then we should follow the example of Jesus and act on it. Not doing so is a major reason a lot of these things never happen in our lives. We can't make what God says come to pass. But we can certainly cooperate with what God has said.

Here are words we find frequently in the Bible. *That it might be fulfilled which was spoken by the prophet.*

There are many things about the Kingdom of Heaven which are still a great secret to the Church. Thankfully, in the past 120 years or so, many of them have been revealed. I expect in the days ahead for many more of them to be revealed.

Interestingly enough these **secrets** are in the Word of God. If we will just open our hearts to understand, the Father will reveal them to us. Granted we may have to think a little differently about certain Scriptures, to understand what God wants to reveal to us in His Word. But it will be more than worth it.

I want to carefully examine the first parable Jesus gave in this series of parables in Matthew chapter 13. After his introductory remarks, Matthew continues with a record of the words and actions of Jesus.

And he spake many things unto them in parables, saying, Behold, a sower went forth to sow; And when he sowed, some seeds fell by the way side, and the fowls came and devoured them up: Some fell upon stony places, where they had not much earth: and forthwith they sprung up, because they had no deepness of earth: And when the sun was up, they were scorched; and because they had no root, they withered away. And some fell among thorns; and the thorns sprung up, and choked them: But other fell into good ground, and brought forth fruit, some an hundredfold, some sixtyfold, some thirty-fold. Who hath ears to hear, let him hear. And the disciples came, and said unto him, Why speakest thou unto them in parables? He answered and said unto them, Because it is given unto you to know the mysteries of the Kingdom of Heaven, but to them it is not given. For whosoever hath, to him shall be given, and he shall have more abundance: but whosoever hath not, from him shall be taken away even that he hath. Therefore speak I to them in parables: because they seeing see not; and hearing they hear not, neither do they understand. And in them is fulfilled the prophecy of Esaias, which saith, By hearing ye shall hear, and shall not understand; and seeing ye shall see, and shall not perceive: For this people's heart is waxed gross, and their ears are dull of hearing, and their eyes they have closed; lest at any time they should see with their eyes and hear with their ears, and should understand with their heart, and should be converted, and I should heal them. But blessed are your eyes, for they see: and your ears, for they hear. For verily I say unto you, That many prophets and righteous men have desired to see those things which ye see, and have not seen them; and to hear those things which ye hear, and have not heard them. (Matthew 13:3-17)

When Jesus had finished telling the parable, the disciples came to Him with a question. They did not ask Jesus to explain the parable. They wanted to know why He was talking to **them** in parables. They made a clear distinction between themselves and the rest of the crowd. What is more important is that Jesus did the same thing. It is the use of the word **them** in the question from the disciples and the answer from Jesus that got my attention. The disciples expected to understand the teaching. Jesus always explained His stories in private. But they wanted to know, "what about **them**?"

Taking notice of this conversation made me curious. Obviously the disciples thought everyone should have the opportunity to understand what Jesus was teaching. Jesus did not agree. The disciples did not have the same view of **them**; the religious crowd, which Jesus had. They saw no reason not to **trust** these people. It had not sunk in; this was the group of people who would later have Jesus crucified. Jesus knew it. Later on He uttered these words.

> *Woe unto the world because of offenses! for it must needs be that offenses come; but woe to that man by whom the offence cometh! (Matthew 18:7)*

A suspect is a person who is thought to be guilty of a crime or offense. Jesus already knew what was going to happen to Him and who would be responsible for it. He had no intention of sharing these precious **secrets** with **them**. They were already plotting against Him and He knew it. He would not fall into their trap. Thus I have chosen to call them, **suspects**.

Jesus was very emphatic in His answer to the disciples. "*It is given unto you to know the mysteries of the Kingdom of Heaven, but to them it is not given.*" I have chosen to be one of those people to whom the **secrets** of the Kingdom of Heaven can be revealed. I believe it is safe to say, since you are reading this book, you have made the same choice. It really is a choice each individual makes. We must decide we want to know these mysteries. Then we must open our hearts to receive them.

In this parable, the **sower** is Jesus. The **secrets** in the story are the **mysteries** of the Kingdom of Heaven which are found in the Word of the Kingdom.

In our world today, we are the sowers. This part has changed. The responsibility to sow the Word of the Kingdom has been transferred from Jesus to us.

What has not changed is the **seed**. The seed is the **container** for the **mysteries** of the Kingdom of Heaven. We often refer to this container as the Word of God.

There are four types of ground, or **soil**, mentioned by Jesus in this parable. They are referred to as the way side, the stony places, among thorns, and good ground.

Four very different things happened to the seed when it was sown into these four very different types of ground. The birds ate some of the seed. The sun scorched some of the seed because there was no root. The thorns choked out some of the seed because the thorns took up more of the ground than the seed placed there by the sower. Finally, the good ground brought forth **fruit**.

You may have noticed Jesus never mentioned any lasting positive results from the seed which fell on the first three types of ground. It was only on the good ground where there were results worth talking about. And even then, the results varied considerably.

There were three different results in the good ground. Each one is defined by the degree to which it produced results. Some of the ground produced a one-hundred-fold return. Other good ground produced a sixty-fold return. Then some only produced a thirty-fold return.

This parable is filled with wonderful secrets.

The very heart of this parable is the **mysteries** of the Kingdom of Heaven. Yet, Jesus never mentioned the Kingdom of Heaven in this parable until the disciples asked him a question. They wanted to know why Jesus was talking to them in parables. Jesus was keeping these **secrets** well hidden from the **suspects**.

Jesus had this wonderful way of saying so much in such a few short words.

Who hath ears to hear, let him hear? Everybody has ears, but they are not all ears to hear. This is very descriptive of where we are today. The spiritual attention span of many people is very short. When a minister is attempting to covey truth which brings understanding, this presents a serious problem. Often people will appear to be listening, but their mind is on something else.

So many people don't have ears to hear. This is another way of describing these first three types of ground. It can be applied to all of the **soil** mentioned in this parable except the soil which produced one-hundred-fold results. Some people only hear what they want to hear.

Hearing what God has to say is an individual choice. Sadly, it is a choice some Christians never make. One of the saddest things I have encountered in the ministry is observing this fact.

I have stood in front of some congregations and wondered why the people were there. I had to work hard to get them to listen. I knew there was a problem. They did not come to church to hear. At times it has seemed as though they did not expect to hear anything which would help them.

Thousands of people stood right in front of Jesus during his three years of public ministry on this earth. Many of them could have cared less about what He had to say. I have to be careful to not be angered by this. I would have loved to sit at Jesus' feet when He was on earth and hear everything He had to say.

Jesus came to this earth to reveal the mysteries of the Kingdom of Heaven. Jesus came to His own people. In this context, we have some very powerful information from the first chapter of the book of John.

He came unto his own, and his own received him not. But as many as received him, to them gave he power to become the sons of God, even to them that believe on his name: Which were born, not of blood, nor of the will of the flesh, nor of the will of man, but of God. (John 1:11-13)

I quote these verses often. It is because of one little phrase which I like to apply to myself. It says: *but as many as received him, to them gave He power to become the sons of God.*

He has given me this power. If you have received Jesus, He has given you this power and we are now sons and daughters of God. **We are not suspects from another kingdom.** We are sons and daughters of the Kingdom of Heaven. We spend our days and even our nights working in the Kingdom of God on this earth. As sons and daughters of God we have one major goal. That goal is to bring as many people as we can into the kingdom. But our work does not stop there.

The rest of our energy is devoted to helping as many people as possible hear and understand these secrets. At the same time we know it is much more than just telling people these things. We must have the help of the Holy Spirit. Only He can bring the necessary revelation.

Chapter Six

No revelation - No results!

———

Jesus knew much of what he said was going to fall on very poor soil. I am referring to those first three types of ground mentioned in this parable. It would not produce good lasting results. These people did not have ears to hear. Therefore, the secrets of the kingdom would not be revealed to them.

It may seem a little harsh for me to express my ideas in this manner. But perhaps another reason Jesus was speaking in parables was so he did not waste any seed. **Why place the seed in soil which would not produce results?**

We only plant seed so it will grow and produce fruit. This is certainly true in the natural realm. Why would it not be true in the spiritual realm? James wrote these words expressing a similar thought.

> *Be patient therefore, brethren, unto the coming*
> *of the Lord. Behold, the husbandman waiteth*
> *for the precious fruit of the earth, and hath*
> *long patience for it, until he receive the early*
> *and latter rain. (James 5:7)*

We literally choose how much of the mysteries of the Kingdom of Heaven will be revealed to us. We decide how much we will benefit from the goodness of God. No one else can stop the blessings of God. It is entirely up to us. We control our ears.

This parable from Matthew chapter 13 has everything to do with who is going to find out about these secrets. Jesus was very clear regarding **who will   not** find out about these secrets. He was just as clear about **who will** know about them.

Please understand it was not as though Jesus came to earth with some predetermined or preordained list of people who would listen to Him. Some people want to believe things work this way in the Kingdom of Heaven. They simply do not work in this way.

Jesus wanted these people to understand. He wanted to give them the **secrets** of the kingdom. Revelation was a great part of His reason for coming to earth. But these people made their choice. It was true at that time in history and people are still making this choice.

When we talk to people about the basic things in the Kingdom of Heaven, we are giving them an opportunity to make a choice. **Many of them do want to hear.** They want to hear much more than we sometimes think they do. This is not always something you can tell by the way people talk and the way they act or look.

The religious people at the synagogues in Jesus' day were the very ones who did not have ears to hear. Religion drove them to the synagogue. It was not their desire to know the **secrets** of the kingdom. They had been working at not hearing the voice of God for a long time. Many of them had a head full of knowledge. But sadly, they were void of understanding. This was especially evident regarding the Son of God.

When Jesus was beginning His earthly ministry, He found twelve men whom we call the disciples. Eleven of these men really wanted to hear what Jesus had to say. They desired to understand who He was and why He was here on earth. This is actually the reason they were called disciples. I said there were only eleven who were true disciples because at some point along the way, **Judas quit hearing.** We know what a mistake this was.

Without realizing what they were doing at the time, these eleven men decided they would be the ones to whom it was given to know the secrets of the kingdom. **Revelation** would be theirs on a daily basis.

As time passed and many wonderful miracles were performed other men and many women joined the group. They decided to be people to whom the secrets of the kingdom would be given. You and I have joined this group. We have decided to be among those to whom the secrets of the kingdom will be revealed.

In case you wonder if I mean by my statements more things will be added to the Bible, let me tell you. The answer is emphatically NO! From this perspective there are no more secrets to be given. All of the mysteries of the kingdom are written in the Scriptures. Nothing needs to be or can be added to it. What we are in serious need of is an understanding of what has already been recorded in the Bible.

Matthew 13:12 is a Scripture which I have found to be both intriguing and very enlightening. Jesus said this.

> *For whosoever hath, to him shall be given, and he shall have more abundance: but whosoever hath not, from him shall be taken away even that he hath.*

This is one of the wonderful secrets of the Kingdom of Heaven. Jesus spoke of it often. In this case He was talking specifically about understanding. Here is another place in the Bible where Jesus used this statement in reference to money.

For the Kingdom of Heaven is as a man traveling into a far country, who called his own servants, and delivered unto them his goods. And unto one he gave five talents, to another two, and to another one; to every man according to his several ability; and straightway took his journey. Then he that had received the five talents went and traded with the same, and made them other five talents. And likewise he that had received two, he also gained other two. But he that had received one went and digged in the earth, and hid his lord's money. After a long time the lord of those servants cometh, and reckoneth with them. And so he that had received five talents came and brought other five talents, saying, Lord, thou deliveredst unto me five talents: behold, I have gained beside them five talents more. His lord said unto him, Well done, thou good and faithful servant: thou hast been faithful over a few things, I will make thee ruler over many things: enter thou into the joy of thy lord. He also that had received two talents came and said, Lord, thou deliveredst unto me two talents: behold, I have gained two other talents beside them. His lord said unto him, Well done, good and faithful servant; thou hast been faithful over a few things, I will make thee ruler over many things: enter thou into the joy of thy lord. Then he which had received the one talent came and said, Lord, I knew thee that thou art an hard man, reaping where thou hast not sown, and gathering where thou hast not strawed: And I was afraid, and went and hid thy talent in the earth: lo, there thou hast that is thine. His lord answered and said unto him, Thou wicked and slothful servant, thou knewest that I reap where I sowed not, and gather where I have not strawed: Thou oughtest therefore to have put my money to the exchangers, and then at my coming I should have received mine own with usury. Take therefore the talent from him, and give it unto him which hath ten talents. For unto every one that hath shall be given, and he shall have abundance: but from him that hath not shall be taken away even that which he hath. (Matthew 25:14-29)

This passage of scripture is one of the most misunderstood and misinterpreted things Jesus ever said. This is not a story about people who can sing and play instruments. Jesus was telling a story about investing money. He was stressing the importance of doing it wisely. This point is made very clear in the rebuke the lord gave to the servant who only had one talent. The lord said to him, "*Thou oughtest therefore to have put my money to the exchangers, and then at my coming I should have received mine own with usury.*"

The words **exchangers** and **usury** need to be defined. These words are often used incorrectly in sermons.

Strong's Concordance states an **exchanger**[1] is a money changer, broker, banker or one who exchanges money for a fee, and pays interest on deposits. The Greek word for **usury**[2] means: interest of money, usury (because it multiplies money, and as it were, breeds).

We often think of usury as an excessive amount of interest being charged. In fact, there are laws against doing such a thing as charging too much interest. This is not what Jesus intended this to mean. He was teaching the concept mentioned in the definition given in the concordance. When money is properly invested it multiplies. **In a real sense money breeds money.** This concept was built into the universe at the time of creation. It is specifically mentioned in these verses.

> *Then God said, "Let the land produce vegetation: seed-bearing plants and trees on the land that bear fruit with seed in it, according to their various kinds." (Genesis 1:11 - NIV)*

> *And God said, "Let the land produce living creatures according to their kinds: the livestock, the creatures that move along the ground, and the wild animals, each according to its kind." And it was so. (Genesis 1:24 - NIV)*

God's plan is for money to make money. Jesus knew this. Jesus was very active in the creation of this earth and everything on it. He expected money to produce (breed) money.

It is man's plan to spend and waste money. It is God's plan for money to be invested and to make money. In order for this to happen a person must have some money with which to start. This is the meaning behind, *For unto every one that hath shall be given, and he shall have abundance: but from him that hath not shall be taken away even that which he hath.*

My favorite dessert is German Chocolate Cake. Any person reading this who has ever made one of these cakes is well aware it takes a lot of time to make one. I am not talking about using a cake mix. When I bake one of these cakes it is made from totally fresh ingredients. The pecans absolutely must be fresh if the icing is going to be as good as you hope it to be. I have made many of these cakes and it has become a family favorite. Perhaps this is because I cover every inch of the cake, including the bottom of it with that delicious icing.

Suppose I announced a meeting for people who would like to make one of these cakes. Included in my announcement would be the fact, I have learned how to keep the cake portion of the cake very moist. It does not dry out like some cakes do. There is a special, albeit very time consuming, way to mix the ingredients of a German Chocolate Cake which gives it the texture I (and apparently a lot of other people) prefer.

I know what would happen if I made an event available to teach people how to make a better German Chocolate Cake. The people who would come to the event would be those who already make this kind of cake. No doubt some of these people are much better at this than I am. These people already **have** something. They have skill and experience and knowledge. However, because of what they **have**, they are seeking ways to **have more**. This is the way successful people think and act.

The people who would not come to my cake event would be those who **do not bake cakes**, especially this one. There may be a person who does bake this kind of cake (**but they are never pleased with the results**) and they probably would not come to hear what I have to say. It is because of **what they do not have** that they will miss out. As Jesus stated, *from him that hath not shall be taken away even that which he hath.*

If a person has money and does invest it as Jesus was teaching, he should expect to gain even more money. Eventually, if he does not at least make some money then something is wrong. He has not put his money in the right place. Or even worse he has placed his money in a scam or with a scoundrel.

Good investing is safer than not investing. The reason is simple and sadly very true. People who do not invest in something invariably wind up with nothing. Far too many people in the United States come to the last few years of their life and live in poverty. In a land so blessed, this should not be the case. But it is an individual choice.

I am not being critical. But the level of poverty among the oldest people in our Nation certainly makes my point.

*From him that hath not shall be taken away
even that which he hath.*

Both sides to this story represent secrets of the Kingdom of Heaven which are not well understood. I have spent years in the Financial Services Industry. I am now retired from this business and no longer hold any licenses. But I have seen first-hand the evidence to back up what I am saying to you.

My prayer is for God to give great understanding to the hearts of believers regarding the right and wise way to handle their money. I want to see people in the Kingdom of God prosper while they still live on this earth.

Often in a joking manner it has been said:
"The rich get richer - and the poor get poorer."

This is true. It is a very realistic outlook. Jesus said

this in so many words. It is all about **what we do with what we have.** It is very sad to see how many poor people experience this phenomenon and never seem to understand why this happens in their life.

Our schools do not teach our children how to handle money in the right way. Perhaps it is because many of the teachers have not been taught. A lot of people live out their lives and never catch on to what really makes the difference. Once again let me say the difference is found in what you do with what you have. This is a powerful secret in the Kingdom of Heaven.

This is what makes the difference in the parable of the sower. It is what makes the difference in the story about the talents. **With regard to the matter of understanding it is all about what you do with your ears.** Do you have ears to hear? Then, what you do with what comes into your ears? Do you act on it? Finally, what do you do with the mysteries of the kingdom after you hear them?

This makes the difference in every area of our lives.

Many people never do anything positive with what they have. There are reasons why this is the case. Here are some of those reasons. They don't know what they have. They don't know how to figure out what they have. They don't know how to do anything with what they have. They don't recognize the favor which is theirs because of what they have. Often they place very little value on what they have. This last reason may be the most damaging.

Instead of doing what they can with what they do have, they convince themselves their life would be so much better if they just had what some other successful person has. Sadly, this is nothing more than a very destructive form of envy. It is a trap. If you have fallen into this trap, now would be a good time to break free.

God places great value on everything He has given to you. God is fully aware of what can become of what He gave to you. He wants to show you. This is a part of the job of the Holy Spirit. We must open our hearts to what the Holy Spirit wants to both tell us and show us.

Place the same value on what you have that God has placed on it. Now let's look further at Matthew 13.

> *And in them is fulfilled the prophecy of Esaias, which saith, By hearing ye shall hear, and shall not understand; and seeing ye shall see, and shall not perceive: For this people's heart is waxed gross, and their ears are dull of hearing, and their eyes they have closed; lest at any time they should see with their eyes and hear with their ears, and should understand with their heart, and should be converted, and I should heal them. (Matthew 13:13-15)*

These verses contain a vivid description of the people of Israel as Jesus found them when He came to this earth. They did this to themselves long before Jesus was born. This is not just my opinion. Jesus was very clear about this when He said. *"Their eyes they have closed; lest at any time they should see with their eyes and hear with their ears, and should understand with their heart."*

Think for a moment about all God had done for the people of Israel. From the time of Abraham, how many miracles had they seen with their eyes – literally? In their history, these people had more direct knowledge of God than anyone had ever been privy to, since the time of Adam. They had the knowledge. And God had spelled out for them how to walk in this knowledge.

God had told them what would happen if they **did** live by what He said to them. He expressly told them what would happen to them, if they **did not** live by what He had told them. Yet, much of this was completely ignored.

Wisdom was offered to them and they refused it. They stopped listening and their ears became dull. Here was the real problem. **This people's heart became gross.**

I have found some very interesting ways to express this same thought in various translations. Some are a little more blunt than others. However, they all are making the same important point.

The Easy to Read Version of the Bible says: "the minds of these people are now closed".

Holman Christian Standard Bible says: "for this people's heart has grown callous".

The Message Bible says: "the people are blockheads"!

The Worldwide English (New Testament) says: "the hearts of these people have no feeling".

This heart problem did not happen overnight. Isaiah prophesied this would happen to the Nation of Israel.

What we see is a reaction from the natural man to things which happened to people who did not have an understanding heart. In spite of their knowledge Israel never understood the **mysteries or secrets** of the Kingdom of Heaven. Here is a warning and great wisdom for us to follow. The choice to understand is an individual matter.

So above all, guard the affections of your heart, for they affect all that you are. Pay attention to the welfare of your innermost being, for from there flows the wellspring of life.
(Proverbs 4:23 - TPT)

The next two verses of the parable of the sower are wonderful positive words to the disciples and to us.

But blessed are your eyes, for they see: and your ears, for they hear. For verily I say unto you, that many prophets and righteous men have desired to see those things which ye see, and have not seen them; and to hear those things which ye hear, and have not heard them. (Matthew 13:16-17)

Your eyes are blessed, for they see. Your ears are blessed for they hear.

Donna and I had the privilege of getting to know a man who had known Smith Wigglesworth and E. W. Kenyon. In fact, when this man was a child, Smith Wigglesworth often stayed in his home. There were other men and women of God who were greatly used of God who also stayed in his home when he was a child.

The man I am speaking of was a very accurate Prophet. In fact, I would consider him to be one of the most accurate people I have ever encountered who operated in the gifts of the Holy Spirit. I am specifically speaking of the word of knowledge and the word of wisdom.

When we were with this man and his wife, we would ask him questions about these great men of God he had known personally. He would only tell us a few things and then he would say, "I don't really want to do the talking. I want to listen to you talk about the Bible. You sound just like these guys you are asking me about when you teach." I was honored greatly but it was also very humbling.

Many times, this man asked me, "what does this or that scripture mean"? "Please tell me more."

This was a very humbling experience. The man was about thirty years older than I was. At the time I was only in my forties. He had spent many years in the ministry and had been in the company of great men of God.

I am not expressing these things to say something about myself. I am making a very important point about this man of God. **This man had ears to hear.** He was very good soil. Spiritually speaking, I would definitely put this man in the category of the one-hundred fold return.

In fact, every great man of God I have had the privilege of knowing, has had ears to hear. They want to know more. Give them a chance and they will try to find out if you have some understanding they do not yet have.

I have always tried to get these wonderful people to talk to me and share what they know. I also have ears to hear. But I have found it is hard to get much out of people who still want to learn. They may talk for a while. However, I have found they are probably setting things up to get something from you. They want to share in the revelation God may have given to you.

For many years, I really did not know what to think about what I am telling you. I always wondered why these great people wanted me to talk when they had so much more to say than I did. Then one day I realized this was the real secret to their greatness in the Kingdom of Heaven.

They never stopped having ears to hear.

They had received an understanding of various mysteries of the Kingdom of Heaven. They all knew many of these secrets and benefited from them, but they always wanted more.

I have come to believe this was the manner in which Jesus spoke of another fruit of the spirit. *The King James Version* calls it **meekness**. You will find many different opinions about the meaning of the word meekness. I certainly am not saying these definitions are incorrect. But I would encourage you to consider a different possibility. Perhaps the word meekness really means to be teachable. A teachable attitude is certainly key to our spiritual growth.

Chapter Seven

A Heart Waxed Gross

———

In my years as a Pastor I have found most Christians are confronted with two major needs. One of these is the need for finances. The other is the need for healing. Often these needs are serious. Of course, this is the plight of most of humanity. I am only saying, this does not seem to change much when people get saved. I believe it should. I believe these things can be different for Christians. But often it doesn't work out this way.

Occasionally I have found a church member who had no financial challenges. It wasn't so much because they had a great deal of money. More often than not, they had learned to manage their money well and be content with what they had. I have known numerous very wealthy people. Some of them had huge financial woes. In spite of what many people think, these wealthy people were not greedy people. They worked hard for what they had.

Simultaneously, I have known of so-called ministers who contrived schemes to squeeze money out of believers. They took advantage of people who were already in great need. This has bothered me deeply. I despise watching charlatans take advantage of naïve Christians. I am talking about men and women who pretend to be doing the work of God. Jesus would never have said and done what some of these people say and do. This is an old problem which has never been dealt with in a successful manner.

The challenges to receiving a healing, which is greatly needed, can vary significantly. One of those challenges has been the issue of whether or not it is God's will to heal the sick today. **After all Jesus suffered in the crucifixion, I find it remarkable anyone could think God does not want them to be well.** It is God's will to heal the sick. However, there is a very intriguing statement found in Matthew chapter 13 which I am compelled to discuss. I want you to see the connection Jesus made in these few words. I encourage you to read this Scripture several times before you go any further.

> *For this people's heart is waxed gross, and their ears are dull of hearing, and their eyes they have closed; lest at any time they should see with their eyes and hear with their ears, and should understand with their heart, and should be converted, and I should heal them. (Matthew 13:15)*

In those statements Jesus gave us a list of **reasons for people not receiving their healing**. Jesus said of the people in His audience, their *"heart is waxed gross."* We must discover what this means.

Jesus went on to say, *"their ears are dull of hearing and their eyes they have closed."* I will attempt to explain this very clearly. Skip over the middle part of the verse and read the last five words. It reads, *"and I should heal them."*

A heart which is **waxed gross** will cause a person to become dull of hearing. It will also bring this person to the place, where it can be correctly said of them, *their eyes they have closed.* Jesus placed the burden on these people for them not receiving their healing.

Jesus was not saying it was an inescapable flaw which caused them to be sick. It was not something with which they had been born. He was saying it was something which they had done to cause them to not receive their healing. It was decisions these people had made which prevented Jesus from healing them.

Jesus never indicated an unwillingness to heal the sick. He honored what was in the heart of the person in need of healing. Jesus often asked what the sick person wanted Him to do. We have turned this around to our own detriment. When we are sick or have a disease we tend to ask God what He wants to do.

God, are you willing to heal me? Is it your will for me to be well? These are the wrong questions. **We should assume God wants us to be well.** What Jesus suffered in the crucifixion leaves no question about where Jesus and the Father stand on the issue of our health and healing. We must bring the questions back to ourselves.

What is the condition of my heart? To use the words Jesus used, is my heart *waxed gross?* What do my eyes see? What are my ears hearing? Have I closed my eyes to my healing? Have my ears become dull?

I have aroused your curiosity about what Jesus said in order to begin talking about a heart with understanding.

One of the major things preventing Christians with sickness and disease from receiving their healing is not having an **understanding heart.** This is what Jesus said. Therefore, I am compelled to help you develop an understanding heart. If I can succeed in this. Then I will have greatly assisted you in receiving your healing.

In order to accomplish this task, I must share with you what it means to have an understanding heart. Only then can I help you grasp what is necessary to have an understanding heart. I really can't take you beyond this point. The remainder of the task will be up to you. Believe me, if I could give you an understanding heart I certainly would.

The key to understanding with our heart is receiving a revelation of the Word of God. This is true with healing. It is true with salvation. I am sure you noticed I skipped over the statement in Matthew 13:15 about being converted. I did this because I am writing to people who are already converted. If you happen not to be a person who is born-again, go back through the pages of this book and you will discover what is necessary to be converted.

I am convinced this matter of revelation is the missing key to many people not receiving what they need and desire from God. They know what the Bible says, and they believe it. But it has never become a revelation to their heart. They do not understand with their heart. I am doing my best to help you have an understanding heart. **An understanding heart is one filled with revelation from God and His Word.**

By **revelation**[1] I mean truth we have not known before and truth our minds would be incapable of knowing without the aid and assistance of the Holy Spirit. Truth is much more than just something being accurate or correct. Truth, real truth, takes on a life of its own.

Consider this verse of Scripture.

> *Jesus answered, "I am the way and the truth and the life. No one comes to the Father except through me." (John 14:6 - NIV)*

71

Jesus told us in this verse, the truth is a person. Jesus is truth. Perhaps one of our problems in developing an understanding heart is how we view this person. I have a concern we may only see Him as a man or as God. We do not tend to see Jesus as **the embodiment of truth.**

I am speaking of something which can only come by revelation. By the use of the word revelation I mean our **mind** is incapable of knowing Jesus for who He really is. We must have the assistance of the Holy Spirit. I am not just speaking about a concept.

We need a greater revelation of Jesus.

I am talking about really knowing Jesus. He is a living, vibrant, loving, healing Jesus. He is literally seated at the right hand of God the Father. We know these things as facts. But does our heart really understand what Jesus did to make them a reality. I can tell you about these things. I may even convince your mind. But only the Holy Spirit can make it real to your **heart.**

Since you are reading this book, I would assume you know a great deal about Jesus and what He has done for you. You do believe in Him. My challenge to you is this. Are these just facts and bits of information? Or, is your healing a revelation to you? What is the condition of your ears? What is the condition of your eyes? What is the condition of your heart? **Is it waxed gross?**

I will change my choice of words. We get so accustomed to hearing certain words regarding these Scriptures they go right past us. They have no more impact than the words of any other book. **The real purpose of revelation is understanding.** Since a lack of understanding with our hearts can keep us from being healed, it naturally follows that a lack of revelation can keep us from being healed. A lack of truth being given to us by the Holy Spirit (which is the essential meaning of revelation) can keep us from being healed. This lack of revelation was withholding healing from the religious crowd.

It seems appropriate to ask the question. Then why were so many people healed during the earthly ministry of Jesus? To me, the answer is simple - yet profound.

The Holy Spirit was at work. This was true both with Jesus and later with Peter, John, Paul, Phillip and many others. The Holy Spirit was revealing to people healing was available to them. In many cases all these people needed to do was touch Jesus in some way. The healing was even resident in His clothes.

Touching Jesus or His clothes is something I have heard discussed many times. There are even songs written about it. The songs try to get people to imagine touching the hem of the robe Jesus wore. This will not do you any good. You can't touch Jesus today. So, Jesus gave us two very powerful alternatives to His physical touch.

These first alternative is having the hands of other believers touch us. We commonly refer to this as laying hands on the sick. The other alternative is to receive a revelation of the Word of God regarding your healing.

The same Holy Spirit who was at work in Jesus is here today to bring revelation to you. He does this through the Word of God.

> ✗ *So Jesus said to the Jews who had believed him, "If you abide in my word, you are truly my disciples, and you will know the truth, and the truth will set you free." (John 8:31-32 - ESV)*

These are very interesting words spoken by Jesus. In one place Jesus declared He is the truth. I spoke of that earlier. In this Scripture Jesus told us how to continue in the truth. Take special note of the connection Jesus has made in His statements regarding His Word and the truth. These two things are inseparable. Knowing this changes many things. Keeping in mind, Jesus is the truth, we can draw these conclusions.

If we want to be set free from anything, such as a sickness or disease we must do the following. We must know the truth. The truth is Jesus. We must know Him.

Knowing Jesus requires a revelation of the Truth. This Truth is found in His Word. We call this the Bible.

To understand this Truth, we must abide in His Word. As we abide in His Word, The Holy Spirit brings the revelation of this Truth we desperately need.

Let's double back to the verse in Matthew 13 with which we began. We can now see all of this requires an understanding heart. We must not have a heart which is in the words of Jesus, *"waxed gross."* **A heart that is waxed gross is one which has no desire nor intent to do the things I just spoke about.** This person has closed their eyes and their ears are dull of hearing.

Strong's Exhaustive Concordance of the Hebrew and English Bible says metaphorically the phrase **waxed gross** means: **to make stupid** (to render the soul dull or callous)[2]. Jesus declared in regard to the multitude that they had made themselves stupid. You probably do not think of Jesus speaking in those terms.

However, any person, then or now who would not want to hear what Jesus has to say could be considered stupid. This was and is the very Son of God. I am not being cruel or mean. What I am saying is consistent with the following verses of Scripture.

The fool hath said in his heart, There is no God. They are corrupt, they have done abominable works, there is none that doeth good. The Lord looked down from Heaven upon the

*children of men, to see if there were any that
did understand, and seek God. They are all
gone aside, they are all together become filthy:
there is none that doeth good, no, not one.
Have all the workers of iniquity no knowledge? who eat up my people as they eat bread,
and call not upon the Lord. (Psalm 14:1-4)*

This may seem harsh to some who read it, but it
is true. We are living in a world with an increasing
number of fools. They say there is no God. All of
these things stated in this Psalm are descriptive of our
world today. I could continue on this theme, but I am
sure you get my point. It was to the descendants of
the people addressed in this Psalm that Jesus declared
they have made themselves stupid. In the most direct
and simple of terms, Jesus was telling it the way it is.

The word **stupid**[3] simply means: having or showing a
great lack of intelligence or common sense.

I can't think of anything which illustrates a lack of
intelligence more than being in the physical presence of
Jesus and not paying close attention to His every word
and action.

I have gone to these great lengths to demonstrate to you
the opposite of what it means to have an understanding
heart. The words waxed gross seem very appropriate.

It is my great desire and determination to have an understanding heart. I want the same for you. Therefore, before I go further, I want to explain something else which may seem at first to be off the subject. I am making reference to people being offended. **Offense** is usually due to a lack of understanding.

The more your understanding heart grows the less likely you will be to get offended. It is not just because you are willing to ignore or overlook things which might offend you. You have received a more complete outlook on human nature. You are more inclined to **forgive**. You recognize character flaws you see in other people. The question arises as to why this would be the case.

On the path to developing an understanding heart you discover more and more of your own flaws. You see them clearly. You also set a course to deal with them so they do not have a negative impact on your life or the lives of other people. This action on your part helps you to realize **others have simply not done what you are in the process of doing**.

At first, you might think this spiritual growth would make you more intolerant. This tends to only be true when people fit the description of Psalm 14, which I just quoted. But even in those cases an understanding heart is accompanied by a spiritual maturity which enables you to quickly move on.

You choose to disassociate yourself with such people rather than hang around them and be offended.

Why is this so important? It is vitally important because **being offended can keep you from receiving your healing.** This is true simply because of what being offended does to your heart. A little later in this book we are going to be looking at what Jesus said about people being offended.

To get to this point I will first lead you through a study of the explanation Jesus gave us regarding the parable of the sower.

Chapter Eight

Soil-sample Analysis

———

Beginning with verse 18 of Matthew chapter 13, Jesus explained the parable of the sower. We will take this one statement at a time and I will attempt to make it as clear as I possibly can.

> *Hear ye therefore the parable of the sower. When any one heareth the Word of the Kingdom, and understandeth it not, then cometh the wicked one, and catcheth away that which was sown in his heart. This is he which received seed by the way side. (Matthew 13:18-19)*

After His introductory statement Jesus made an interesting comment which I do not ever recall hearing anyone address. Jesus said: *"When any one heareth the Word of the Kingdom."* It really makes me wonder what Jesus meant by this remark.

Several thoughts occur to me. I have written about the mysteries (or as I have called them the secrets) of the Kingdom of Heaven. Now we have mention of the Word of the Kingdom. What is the **Word of the Kingdom?** Perhaps I should ask the question in this way.

Does the Kingdom of Heaven have its own language? Is this what Jesus was talking about? Or, did Jesus mean there are certain things which are acceptable to say in this kingdom and certain words which are not to be said? Let's consider this possibility.

In the Kingdom of God, which is on this earth, there is a **manual** which tells us everything we need to know to function in the kingdom. This manual also tells us all we really need to know to be successful on this earth. I do not mean it gives us specific data about every area of our lives. I am saying this manual gives us the **principles** and the **broad guidelines** to follow. The Holy Spirit fills in the details as we follow His voice and guidance.

By now you have surely guessed I am talking about the Bible. Many people know it as the **Word of God.** And whether we have made the connection or not, we have given the Bible this name because it is the **Word of the Kingdom.** This is where we get the **seed** Jesus spoke of in this parable. Without doubt we believe the Word of God is the most important way in which God speaks to us as believers.

We preach and we teach the Word of God. We pray and we say the Word of God. It is not just another book. It is a living document. Hearing what the Word of God says and acting on it has changed our lives. It is the Word of the Kingdom.

There are several things revealed in the explanation to the parable of the sower to help us discover the secrets of the kingdom. Jesus taught us several different ways the Devil keeps people from discovering these mysteries. Then Jesus revealed the most important factor to discovering the mysteries of the kingdom. All of this is contained in this parable and is made even more clear in the explanation which Jesus gave of the parable.

Here is an outstanding set of instructions God gave to Israel through the mouth of Moses. We probably will not literally do what these instructions say and strap a leather box on our head. But the **principal** contained in these words has great value in our world.

Take heed to yourselves, that your heart be not deceived, and ye turn aside, and serve other gods, and worship them; And then the Lord's wrath be kindled against you, and he shut up the Heaven, that there be no rain, and that the land yield not her fruit; and lest ye perish quickly from off the good land which the Lord giveth you. Therefore shall ye lay up these my

*words in your heart and in your soul, and
bind them for a sign upon your hand, that
they may be as frontlets between your eyes.
And ye shall teach them your children, speaking of them when thou sittest in thine house,
and when thou walkest by the way, when thou
liest down, and when thou risest up. And thou
shalt write them upon the door posts of thine
house, and upon thy gates: That your days may
be multiplied, and the days of your children,
in the land which the Lord sware unto your
fathers to give them, as the days of Heaven
upon the earth. (Deuteronomy 11:16-21)*

Jesus knew this passage of Scripture. He may have
even quoted the entire portion in one of His many
teachings. His disciples and many of His audience knew
these instructions as well. On the other hand, it is sad to
say many Gentile Christians have never been taught the
most basic elements found in these verses.

They do not understand these things about the God
we love and serve. They do not know God's will and His
plan for their life on this earth is good. And I do mean
really good people. Any person who does not have a good
life cannot correctly point a finger of blame at God. **It is
never His fault.** They may try, but they are wrong. The
keys or perhaps I should say the plans for this life are
given to us in the Scriptures.

God spoke these words to Israel. He was telling them there is a way to live a wonderful life on this planet in spite of the fall of man. God even went so far as to call this *"days of Heaven upon the earth."* I would go so far as to say **it is the will of God for us to begin enjoying the Kingdom of Heaven now!** Yes, I do mean while we are still living on this earth.

What would bring these days of Heaven on earth?

It starts with each of us as individuals. This is always the case. Before we look at anyone else, we are told to *take heed to yourselves, that your heart be not deceived.* Take heed to yourself. You are responsible for you. I know in today's world this is really a radical idea.

Irresponsible behavior is at an all time high. In all the years I have been alive, I do not believe I have witnessed anything quite like it. Everything is someone else's fault. Lawsuits over the most minor of things is commonplace. This failure to accept responsibility leads to a serious heart condition. The writer tells us why we must take heed to ourselves. It is for this reason: *That your heart be not deceived.*

Irresponsibility leads to deception of the heart. The proof is all around us. More than irresponsible behavior, I witness the deception in the hearts of so many of the young people in our society. I know there can be a tendency among young people to do stupid and reckless things. It happened when I was young. But there was a difference, which I do not see much of today, which is very disturbing. Most of us grew up and put away our foolishness.

So many young leaders in the world today have not grown up. We have a number of them in Congress. Their hearts are deceived. They find it acceptable to defy the basic elements of humanity. There is a push to pass laws which would completely change the United States of America. If they succeed it will ultimately make this nation more like a third world country. If you think I am exaggerating, you have not been paying attention. I will express my sentiments in one verse of Scripture.

> *Righteousness exalteth a nation: but sin is a reproach to any people. (Proverbs 14:34)*

Being **irresponsible** leads to a **deceived** heart. A deceived heart leads to **rebellion** against authority; both man's authority and God's authority. Rebellion leads to **sin.** Sin is a reproach to any people. The only way to correct this is to follow the path of righteousness.

The pathway back to righteousness does not begin with only accepting responsibility for myself. The first step is **repentance.** America has a huge sin problem. Sadly some ministers are teaching against repentance. They say it isn't something a Christian needs to do. This is dangerous!

The church has been too busy telling people how good they are. I am not for putting people down and beating them over the head with the Bible. But we must **get over our fear of calling sin what it is.** No matter how much people want to change our society, the Word does not change and it will not change. We must have a society norm based on the Word of the Kingdom.

The following words are still just as true as they have ever been. This is the pathway to righteousness. This is the way back.

> *If my people, which are called by my name, shall humble themselves, and pray, and seek my face, and turn from their wicked ways; then will I hear from Heaven, and will forgive their sin, and will heal their land. (2 Chronicles 7:14)*

Only you and I can keep our hearts from being deceived. Avoiding deception is totally an individual responsibility. No one else can do it for you. Consider the following statements from the book of James.

> *Wherefore, my beloved brethren, let every man be swift to hear, slow to speak, slow to wrath: For the wrath of man worketh not the righteousness of God. Wherefore lay apart all filthiness and superfluity of naughtiness, and*

receive with meekness the engrafted word, which is able to save your souls. But be ye doers of the word, and not hearers only, deceiving your own selves. For if any be a hearer of the word, and not a doer, he is like unto a man beholding his natural face in a glass: For he beholdeth himself, and goeth his way, and straightway forgetteth what manner of man he was. But whoso looketh into the perfect law of liberty, and continueth therein, he being not a forgetful hearer, but a doer of the work, this man shall be blessed in his deed. If any man among you seem to be religious, and bridleth not his tongue, but deceiveth his own heart, this man's religion is vain. Pure religion and undefiled before God and the Father is this, To visit the fatherless and widows in their affliction, and to keep himself unspotted from the world. (James 1:19-27)

What great instructions for our times we find in these verses. James has laid out so very clearly the very things I have been writing. We must do the things we know to do.

Any individual who hears the Word and does not do it deceives himself. I love the illustration James has given. He depicts the Word of the Kingdom as a mirror. Very few people have never looked in **this mirror**. It is still true the Bible has been printed more times than any other book in history. This alone tells us many people are searching for answers.

There are numerous stories and even detailed articles on the Internet regarding the numbers of Bibles which have been printed. In those I checked the second book in the list was not even a close second.

My point is not to argue the specific facts regarding how many Bibles there are in the world. I only want to emphasize the matter of its **availability** in all of its forms. No other book has ever been spoken about as publicly on the radio, on television and now on the Internet as the Bible. The world has had the **opportunity to look in the mirror.** Thank God for those billions of people who have looked and have done what this great Word instructs us to do. The sad part is the number of people who have looked in the mirror and walked away unchanged. They did nothing with what they saw and the result is self-deception.

James 1:26 is very powerful. *If any man among you seem to be religious, and bridleth not his tongue, but deceiveth his own heart, this man's religion is vain.*

James has settled the issue. People can seem to be religious, but they have not changed. The most telling proof is their inability to control their tongue. **Their words reveal they have deceived their own heart.**

This is religious vanity!

The writer of the book of Proverbs has this to say.

> *You are snared by the words of your mouth;*
> *You are taken by the words of your mouth.*
> *(Proverbs 6:2 - NKJV)*

Our words reveal our true character. I must take responsibility for myself. If I keep my heart from being deceived there are a number of things I will do. According to what God told Israel in the passage I quoted from the book of Deuteronomy the following will be an outline for my life.

- I will not go after other gods.
- I will lay up His Words in my heart and in my soul.
- I will keep His Word always around me.
- It will be in my hands and in front of my eyes. I am glad it is a book and not a scroll.
- I will teach the Word of the Kingdom to my children.
- I will teach my children at home. I will not leave the spiritual nourishing of my children to somebody else.
- No matter where I am, I will be talking about the Word.
- I will have things visibly displayed in my house on the walls and on the shelves with scriptures on them.
- May I just say, your house is not properly decorated if you don't see Scriptures on display in your house in some form.

No, this is not extreme. It is not radical. At least it is not radical if you consider yourself to be a part of the Kingdom of God. It is not radical if you consider the Bible to be the Word of God. These things should be your automatic reaction and not a legalistic response. It should be your heart's response to who you are.

Doing these things I just listed demonstrates we understand, the Word of the Kingdom holds the keys to the mysteries of the Kingdom of Heaven. These words are the secret to days of Heaven on earth. This is the path to enjoying what God intended for us in this life. Make the Word a very real part of your life. If you do not understand much of what you read in the Bible, there is a reason. The solution is learning to benefit from the work of the Holy Spirit. Jesus gave us this insight:

> *Howbeit when he, the Spirit of truth, is come, he will guide you into all truth: for he shall not speak of himself; but whatsoever he shall hear, that shall he speak: and he will shew you things to come. (John 16:13)*

A great part of the work of the Holy Spirit is bringing **revelation** and **understanding** into our lives. The difference between: Hell on earth and Heaven on earth is understanding these mysteries of the Kingdom. The only way to understand these **secrets** is to gain a better understanding of the Word.

This is precisely the purpose of this book. I have accepted the assignment of doing my best to help you have an understanding heart. I can now finish the first statement Jesus made explaining this parable.

> When any one heareth the Word of the
> Kingdom, and understandeth it not, then
> cometh the wicked one, and catcheth away
> that which was sown in his heart. This
> is he which received seed by the way side.
> (Matthew 13:19)

Jesus was informing the disciples the Devil comes to people who have no understanding. **People who have no understanding are his number one target.** This does not mean the Devil does not come to people who do have understanding. We know from our experience he certainly does. However, the Devil prefers an easier target. This is one of the secrets of the kingdom.

One way to get the Devil to leave you alone is to continually grow in your understanding of the Word, and become a person with an understanding heart.

Anyone who is familiar with the story of creation knows the Devil (the serpent) first tempted Eve with the fruit from the tree of knowledge of good and evil. It was then Eve who gave Adam of this fruit after she had eaten of it. Why did the serpent approach Eve first?

For Adam was first formed, then Eve. And Adam was not deceived, but the woman being deceived was in the transgression. (1 Timothy 2:13-14)

Adam was created before Eve. Adam had specific instructions from God. He was told what to do and what not to do. All of this happened before Eve was created. This means **Adam had knowledge and understanding Eve did not have.** Adam should have shared these things with Eve. Obviously this is something he failed to do.

Deception can only occur when a person does not have knowledge. It is almost impossible to deceive a person with understanding. This is the reason it is so easy to deceive small children. It is one reason why we protect our children with great care from people we do not know.

Once you understand the greatest tool the Devil has is the art of deception, it is easy to grasp the message Jesus was giving his disciples. Make certain you have an understanding heart. Shield and protect yourself from the deceptive tactics of your enemy. The wicked one is aware you are hearing the Word.

It is as though Jesus was telling His disciples, "you and everyone else who hears the Word of the Kingdom are a target." This most certainly is a fact. The question to be answered is what are we doing about this?

The secret is in these words; understandeth it not.

The difference in the success or failure of the wicked one is found in the level of understanding in the heart of the hearer of the Word. People who do understand the Word of the Kingdom do fall prey to Satan. They do get involved in sin. However, it is not the result of deception. It is a choice they make.

Here is a Scripture familiar to most Christians.

> *Submit yourselves therefore to God. Resist the Devil, and he will flee from you. (James 4:7)*

These are great and encouraging instructions. But what does it mean to submit yourself to God? How are we supposed to resist the Devil? I believe this is the best answer to both questions. **Develop an understanding heart.**

By its very nature an understanding heart is submitted to God. When we have real understanding of our Father and how He looks at us, it is easy to submit to Him. This is especially true the better we understand who we are and who God wants us to become.

Resisting the Devil does not mean yelling and screaming at him. He is not a natural person and therefore does not respond to natural things. **In the realm where**

the wicked one resides only one thing has power and influence. This is the power of the Word. By the use of your own words the Devil can quickly tell how much you understand the Word of God.

The Devil is terrified of the Word of the Kingdom. This is one of the **secrets** of the kingdom. Heaven knows this. Heaven has seen this Word in action against the Devil. It is no secret to Heaven and it should be no secret to us. Obvious understanding of the Word of the Kingdom is very frightening to the Devil.

We have a tremendous weapon at our disposal. It is the Word of God. This is our greatest weapon. Paul spoke of this great weapon in the following verses. In fact it is the only weapon he mentions in this passage.

> *Wherefore take unto you the whole armor of God, that ye may be able to withstand in the evil day, and having done all, to stand. Stand therefore, having your loins girt about with truth, and having on the breastplate of righteousness; And your feet shod with the preparation of the gospel of peace; Above all, taking the shield of faith, wherewith ye shall be able to quench all the fiery darts of the wicked. And take the helmet of salvation, and the sword of the Spirit, which is the word of God: (Ephesians 6:13-17)*

All but one piece of this armor is defensive in nature. This is not a bad thing. It says we are well equipped from a defensive standpoint against our enemy. We are only given one weapon. It is the only weapon we need for offense against the Devil.

Paul called this the sword of the Spirit. What a great name for the Word of God.

If the Devil is a problem to you, get in the Word. Sharpen your sword. Get a better understanding of what the Word says about you.

The very best way to rebuke the Devil is having an understanding heart. **You will have succeeded before you ever open your mouth.**

In the explanation Jesus gave in Matthew 13:19 Jesus said this Word was sown in the person's heart. We have been trying to function with a great deal of misconception. I am speaking of the matter of the Word of God going into a person's heart when it is taught or preached.

I have heard it said many times; when the Word goes forth it first goes into a person's heart. Obviously from what Jesus said this is correct. This is not the misconception I am speaking of. What I have observed is something which I have found rather disturbing. It is an assumption which is incorrect and dangerous.

We have spoken and acted as though the Word is safe once it reaches the person's heart. The truth is, we have often been perplexed by what we saw happen in the lives of people whom we are certain have heard much of the Word of God. Jesus explained what we have witnessed in this parable.

The safety and security of the Word in a person is determined by the level of understanding the person has of the Word they receive. Too much time has been wasted giving people facts and information. A lot of people have a great deal of knowledge of the Word with precious little understanding of what they know. This is not only sad, it is dangerous. The danger lies in the possibility of deception. A greater danger lies in what the wicked one can do because of this lack of understanding.

Jesus actually said: *"then cometh the wicked one, and catcheth away that which was sown in his heart."*

X Just because the Word gets sown into your heart does not mean you understand it. The opposite is actually true. Understanding is at least a two-step process. God gave Israel these very specific instructions. *"lay up these my words in your heart and in your soul."* *(Deuteronomy 11:18)*

That is a reference to your heart and your mind. Understanding not only involves your heart it also involves your mind. This works in somewhat of a cyclical fashion. I will explain what this means and how it works.

First the Word of the Kingdom goes into your heart. Then by meditating on what is in your heart, your mind becomes engaged. This is what Paul called the renewing of the mind.

As our minds are renewed, we have a greater understanding of the Word which is in our heart. Then the process starts all over with this renewed understanding in our heart. We meditate on this better understanding of the Word in our heart and further renewal of our mind occurs. This is a process which should never stop. It has several names.

We may call it growing spiritually. Spiritual maturity is another name we use. Paul referred to it in another interesting fashion. He called it **perfecting** the saints.

> *And he gave some, apostles; and some, prophets; and some, evangelists; and some, pastors and teachers; For the perfecting of the saints, for the work of the ministry, for the edifying of the body of Christ: Till we all come in the unity of the faith, and of the knowledge of the Son of God, unto a perfect man, unto the measure of the stature of the fulness of Christ: That we henceforth be no more children, tossed*

to and fro, and carried about with every wind
of doctrine, by the sleight of men, and cunning
craftiness, whereby they lie in wait to deceive;
But speaking the truth in love, may grow up
into him in all things, which is the head,
even Christ: From whom the whole body fitly
joined together and compacted by that which
every joint supplieth, according to the effectual
working in the measure of every part, maketh
increase of the body unto the edifying of itself
in love. (Ephesians 4:11-16)

Jesus gave five gifts to the church for the specific purpose of bring perfection to the Body of Christ. This perfection can be seen as having an understanding heart.

The goal is to no longer be children. Remember the earmark of a child is their lack of understanding. In the Ephesian passage we find these words in verse 15: *grow up into him in all things.* **This is what I am calling an understanding heart.** I do not consider the **process** of renewing our minds as spiritual maturity. Rather, spiritual maturity is the **results of this process.** The ultimate goal is to no longer live like spiritual babies.

The Devil does not, and I believe he can not talk to your heart. The Devil talks to your mind. The mind of man is his arena. If your mind is void of understanding with regard to what is in your heart your mind is defenseless against the Devil. Your mind does not have a powerful and effective response to what the Devil says to you.

What I have just expressed may seem to be great assertions. I base them in part on a comment I found in the *Strong's Concordance*. *Strong* says the word **understand**[1] in Matthew 13:19 means to set or join together in the mind.

This is exactly what I have just described.

Here is another bit of information from *Strong's Concordance*. He defines the word **catcheth**[2] as meaning to seize, or to carry off by force. The picture of this person with no understanding is one of persons who have no defense at all. **The Word in their heart has not been joined together in their mind.**

This is the person who received seed by the way side. This individual does not have an understanding heart.

Chapter Nine

The Second Soil-sample Analyzed

———

As Jesus continued His explanation of the parable about the sower, He turned His attention to the seed sown in stony places. He had this to say.

> *But he that received the seed into stony places, the same is he that heareth the word, and anon with joy receiveth it; Yet hath he not root in himself, but dureth for a while: for when tribulation or persecution ariseth because of the word, by and by he is offended. (Matthew 13:20-21)* ·

In each case in this parable these people were receptive to the Word of the Kingdom. None of them outright rejected what the Word of God has to say. In the first three examples Jesus gave in the parable the real problem was with the **soil**.

What intrigues me is the fact Jesus was addressing something which can be resolved, if we make the right effort. In most cases it is not difficult.

The first thing I notice about the second group of people is they received the Word with joy. I have witnessed this many times over the years I have spent in ministry. Numerous individuals have approached me after I spoke and were excited about what I had just taught. A lot of these people attended the churches where I was Pastor. A common statement I heard them declare was, "this is exactly what I have been looking for in a church." Long ago I lost count of how many of these people I never saw or heard from again. I often wondered why. Jesus' explanation of the parable clarifies this for me.

The core reason is found in these seven words: *yet hath he not root in himself.* My reaction to this statement is three-fold. Does he have any roots at all? If so, since those roots are not in himself, where are his roots? Then I must ask why doesn't he have roots in himself?

Mark recorded a slightly different version of the explanation of this parable. He used some wording which provides additional insight. It reads this way.

> *And some fell on stony ground, where it had not much earth; and immediately it sprang up, because it had no depth of earth: But when the*

*sun was up, it was scorched; and because it
had no root, it withered away. (Mark 4:5-6)*

Parallels can be drawn between the way things happen in the natural realm and in the spiritual realm. This is what Jesus was doing when He spoke this parable. He was talking to people who were very familiar with growing things in the dirt. It may not make sense to anyone who has never planted anything, but shallow planting can produce results quicker than deep planting of seeds. This does not mean the results are better. It means there is not a well-developed root system.

Jesus was making the point in a very succinct manner. The real problem was with the soil. **There was no depth to the dirt.** It was stony ground. There was no opportunity for the plant to put down good roots. **Good healthy roots require good soil.**

I don't know much about planting things in the ground, such as trees or plants or flowers. I love a beautiful landscape. I just don't want to do all the work involved in creating one. But I have removed my share of things other people had planted. Occasionally it was vegetation which just grew on its own. I know having strong roots makes all the difference in the world in how well something grows. The root system determines in great part how strong and healthy the plant is going to be. The roots also have much to do with what a plant can endure.

The soil in which something is planted has a lot to do with the ability of most plants to put down roots and grow. **Good soil produces good roots and good plants.**

A few years ago when I began making trips to Pennsylvania to hold meetings in various churches I was intrigued by the countryside. I spent a lot of time in farming communities speaking in smaller churches.

In Pennsylvania there are miles of fence made out of rocks. Even the large corner post is often made of rocks. It appears hundreds of rocks have been placed in a large circular device made of fence wire to form the post.

Considering all the fences I saw, there must be millions of rocks just stacked up to make these fences. Some of them are very long, perhaps more than a mile in length. They appear to not only be everywhere, but to have been there a very long time. Men and women and children **cleared these rocks** out of the fields so they could plant crops and have **good soil** for the crops to put down **roots.**

There is more than one purpose for roots. This is true of natural plants and it is true of spiritual plants.

The prophet Isaiah was quoted frequently by the Lord Jesus. One of my favorite Scriptural quotes is found in the book of Isaiah. When Jesus quoted this passage He stopped in the middle of verse 2.

The Spirit of the Lord God is upon me; because the Lord hath anointed me to preach good tidings unto the meek; he hath sent me to bind up the brokenhearted, to proclaim liberty to the captives, and the opening of the prison to them that are bound; To proclaim the acceptable year of the Lord, and the day of vengeance of our God; to comfort all that mourn; To appoint unto them that mourn in Zion, to give unto them beauty for ashes, the oil of joy for mourning, the garment of praise for the spirit of heaviness; that they might be called trees of righteousness, the planting of the Lord that he might be glorified. (Isaiah 61:1-3)

This is the quote from the book of Luke.

The Spirit of the Lord is upon me, because he hath anointed me to preach the gospel to the poor; he hath sent me to heal the broken-hearted, to preach deliverance to the captives, and recovering of sight to the blind, to set at liberty them that are bruised, To preach the acceptable year of the Lord. And he closed the book, and he gave it again to the minister, and sat down. And the eyes of all them that were in the synagogue were fastened on him. (Luke 4:18-20)

I have taken the time and space to show you this difference in these two passages to be true to the text. Jesus knew He was about to create a real stir among the people with the part He quoted. Obviously, Jesus was making the point these verses were about Him. If at this point in time Jesus had begun to elaborate on the vengeance of our God, things may have become more difficult.

Another reason I called your attention to these verses in Isaiah is to point out to you, we are called: *trees of righteousness, the planting of the Lord.* Jesus wants His trees to be planted in **good soil**. He wants His planting to have a **good root system**.

You may receive the Word with joy. This is great and wonderful. It makes you an excellent part of the audience. It is more fun and it is easier to teach and to preach when people are happy. **But if you don't clear the rocks out of your life you will never be the kind of soil you need to be.** The Word will never take root in your life.

It should be obvious why this is so important. In the natural world I am not sure any crop reaches the harvest without some trouble. It may be severe rain or wind or hail. It may be insects. In this parable Jesus made reference to the sun. It does not have to be anything severe or catastrophic. Just common everyday things like the sun coming up every morning and its rays beating down on a crop with no roots can cause a lot of damage.

So very often I have watched as two people in a congregation went through almost identical things in their lives. I am talking about common, ordinary issues. One of them acted as though it was nothing and the other was in panic mode. The first one paid almost no attention to what was happening. The second one required a lot of the pastor's time just to survive.

The difference was the soil. One was good soil and had produced roots. The second was held in place because on occasion I allowed them to rely on my root structure to keep them from being blown away. To any Pastor who reads this I want to make something very clear.

You may do what I just described because you love the people whom you Pastor. This is why I have done it. I also hope you have learned or will learn the same lesson I did before this destroys you. There is a serious limit to how much of this you can do and survive. It has everything to do with what happens to many Pastors. This is why they burn out. This is why they go to an early grave. It is why they quit the ministry.

God intended for you to help your members **fix their soil**. He never called you to allow people to survive off your spiritual root system.

Most people think of the root system of plants as being the method by which the plants take in moisture and the nutrients the plant needs to grow and produce a good harvest. This certainly is the case. But also, in the parable and in other things Jesus said, **survival is a major reason to have good roots in good soil.**

Jesus said this about our lives.

> *These things I have spoken unto you, that in me ye might have peace. In the world ye shall have tribulation: but be of good cheer; I have overcome the world. (John 16:33)*

If I only consider this one verse of Scripture, I might conclude a warning from Jesus about tribulation is supposed to result in peace. **This would be a wrong.** The peace comes from the things Jesus had already said. The peace comes from the promise of the Holy Spirit. The peace comes from the work of the Holy Spirit. The peace comes from the fact we can ask anything of the Father in the name of Jesus and He will do it.

Peace is one of those roots. I know peace is a fruit of the spirit. But in a very real sense, the type of roots a tree has determines the kind of fruit you will find on the tree. Apple roots do not produce oranges. You can figure out what kind of roots a tree has by the kind of fruit it produces. This is also true in the spiritual realm. I saw an advertisement one time which seems to fit. Some guy said, "deeper roots produce sweeter fruit."

Some people seem to think we can grow enough in faith where we will not have tribulation. They hope for a life with little or no difficulty. Jesus did not teach this because it is not true. Jesus said we will have tribulation. Then he said to be of good cheer.

I want to be very clear Jesus was not saying the tribulation should cause us to be of good cheer. **Trouble does not make you happy unless there is something seriously wrong with the way you think.** You may love a good challenge. You may be bold enough to not back away from difficulty. These are good and admirable traits. But tribulation is never the cause or the source of cheer.

The cheer in our lives comes from the fact Jesus has overcome the world. How is this helpful to us?

In simple terms we benefit from what Jesus has done.

I made a point earlier about allowing others to benefit from my root system. I am greatly limited in how much of this I can do. The same is true for any Pastor. This only works for a very short period of time. It was never intended to be a part of a Pastor's ministry gift. On the other hand, there is no limit where Jesus is concerned. In fact, our ability to grow roots is the result of who we are in Him. We are connected to Him. On one occasion Jesus described our relationship with Him in terms of a vine and its branches.

I am the vine, ye are the branches: He that abideth in me, and I in him, the same bringeth forth much fruit: for without me ye can do nothing. (John 15:5)

His roots are our roots. This is why Jesus was so concerned about these types of soil. Jesus and the church are one whole. We are inseparable. What happens to us is a reflection back on Jesus. What Jesus has already done benefits us.

Jesus said He has overcome the world. John also said something about us overcoming the world.

For whatsoever is born of God overcometh the world: and this is the victory that overcometh the world, even our faith. (1 John 5:4)

We must use our own faith to have this victory. We overcome the world by using our faith. God will not do this for us.

God did not clear the fields in Pennsylvania of those rocks. Those farmers and their families did it so they could grow crops. The kingdom works in a similar fashion. He will not clear our lives of the rocks we are dealing with. **We must remove the rocks.** We are the only ones who can do this. Sadly, this is where a lot of Christians miss it. They are waiting on God to improve the **soil.**

The people who do not clear the **rocks** out of their **soil** will fall prey to the trials and tribulations which come in this life. This will happen no matter how much joy they had when they heard the Word. Look around you. You know people this very thing has happened to.

Not understanding these **secrets** of the kingdom is why so many people have backed away from the Word of the Kingdom. They do not want to hear more.

It certainly does not make me happy to say this, but some of the most profound words Jesus spoke to our generation are found in this part of the parable.

> *but dureth for a while: for when tribulation or persecution ariseth because of the word, by and by he is offended. (Matthew 13:20-21)*

Tribulation and persecution are arising because of the Word. The Devil never sits by and just allows the Word of the Kingdom to go unchallenged. He knows he can't win unless we allow it. Nevertheless, he is willing to test us to see how deep our roots have grown.

What I have found to be so sad and disappointing is the results of this testing by the Devil. Untold thousands of people are offended. It seems like we live in an offended society. The popular solution to this has been something called political correctness.

For the most part this is just a clever tool used by liberals to manipulate people. I have often expressed the application of these next few words to our society.

> *Woe unto them that call evil good, and good evil; that put darkness for light, and light for darkness; that put bitter for sweet, and sweet for bitter! Woe unto them that are wise in their own eyes, and prudent in their own sight! (Isaiah 5:20-21)*

Invariably this describes what happens with people who get **offended**. It brings great confusion to their minds. It turns their world upside down. This is why it is so hard to reach them. **They have chosen to view things in a way opposite to the rest of the people around them.**

Jesus made it clear **the rocks in the soil** of this second group of people were there mostly as **a direct result of being offended.** There were **no roots** because there were **too many rocks.** To a great degree, the **rocks** can be thought of as the **offenses.**

This is very important, so I want to be as clear as I can possibly be. I have known of people who thought they would be wealthy because of their faith. They believed it would happen with great ease. It was their plan to never work another day. Some person convinced them this is the purpose of faith. They embraced this idea with great joy. They held these ideas up as an earmark of their faith. These notions are not founded on the Word of God. These people got offended when it did not happen.

It is the will of God for us to prosper. I have no doubt about this. It is the truth. It is Scriptural. But these things do not happen to any of us in some magical, automatic fashion. They require us to do our part.

The Apostle Paul was very clear when he wrote:

> *For even when we were with you, this we commanded you, that if any would not work, neither should he eat. (2 Thessalonians 3:10)*

The Apostle Paul believed people should work. In the same letter to the Church in Thessalonica, Paul expanded these thoughts about working when he gave these instructions to the people.

> *But as touching brotherly love ye need not that I write unto you: for ye yourselves are taught of God to love one another. And indeed ye do it toward all the brethren which are in all Macedonia: but we beseech you, brethren, that ye increase more and more; And that ye study to be quiet, and to do your own business, and to work with your own hands, as we commanded you; That ye may walk honestly toward them*

> *that are without, and that ye may have lack of*
> *nothing. (1 Thessalonians 4:9-12)*

Many statements in the Word make it clear our prosperity is tightly connected to what we do. **Work does not circumvent our faith.** The two must always go together. In fact, the work we do each day can become a visible expression of our faith. We are not working because we do not expect the blessing of God. We are working because it is one avenue through which God can bless us. Yet, many have become offended never realizing it was due to only trying to benefit from their faith without doing the work God provided.

Offenses (rocks) have been placed in the **soil** due to many different things. Interestingly enough most of these offenses fall into one of the two categories I mentioned at the start of this chapter. The offense can manifest in different ways, but it invariably has to do with money or health issues.

Many people have asked these questions. Why didn't God heal me? He has healed other people with the same problem. Why haven't I gotten a new house? Someone I know, who does not live right got a new house. Why do sinners get raises and promotions and I lost my job?

Many people are hurt and offended by these very things. **These are rocks** we can't afford to have in our lives.

Clear the field - remove the rocks - improve the dirt!

Don't decide the Word of God is not true because you wanted something and have not received it. Hearing the Word alone is not enough. You must understand the Word to benefit from it. Just because the Word goes into your heart when you hear it, this does not mean you understand it. The Word of the Kingdom must have an effect on your heart and your soul; your spirit and your mind.

If you have discovered you are offended, I would like to offer this help to you. Ask yourself this question and be honest when you answer it. **Have I have expected God to do something for me because He did it for someone else?**

God never does anything for one person just because He did it for another. What God does is keep His Word. He keeps His promises. God is not obligated to keep my word. That is my responsibility. I must keep my promises.

We must never base our faith on what God has done for some other person. This is the wrong source of faith. This is true no matter how wonderful and successful that person may be.

I must have faith in what God has said. I must have faith in what God has said to me. I must have faith in what

God has promised me. I must increase my understanding of the Word. Increasing my understanding of The Word of the Kingdom is essential to having an accurate grasp of what God has promised to me.

As simple as all of these statements may sound, these are the **mysteries (secrets)** of the kingdom.

Being offended is like building a wall between you and the mysteries of the kingdom. You can't see over the wall. You can't see anything but the wall. The secrets of the kingdom stay hidden from you. **Tear down the wall. Get rid of the offenses. Improve the dirt!**

Chapter Ten

Who Is Responsible?

———

The skill with which Jesus constructed this parable is amazing. The number of people in each group gets smaller as we progress through the types of soil. Each thing Jesus mentions as causing a problem with the soil is more complex. Each attack of Satan is a more craftily planned than the previous one. No wonder Jesus called this the mysteries of the kingdom. He was exposing the tactics and the plans of the Devil. And did you notice **the Devil's attack is against the Word** of the Kingdom?

Let's take a close look at what a lack of understanding has done to our nation. In my opinion, The United States is the greatest nation on earth. Yet, this great country is reeling under the weight of sin. It all starts with people being robbed of their core values. A complete lack of understanding of the Word of God ultimately can cause people to not know the difference between right and wrong. The deeper this goes into any society the more vile and pagan the people become. Sadly, this describes several cities of the United States. Never did I dream I would see pictures of an American city which reminded me of scenes I have witnessed in third world countries. Yet, it is happening.

When I think back to the parable I have been sharing with you I see the following things. All four of these groups of people heard the Word. The sower was speaking the Word of God to them. The sower was not the ground or the soil. The people hearing the Word were the ground. A few of them were much better ground than the others. **This is a parable about understanding what we hear.** We hear all sorts of things everyday but what we must hear is the Word of the Kingdom. And most importantly we must understand what we hear.

Regarding soil sample #1: Jesus told us their problem was one of being completely **void of understanding.** This is the largest group of people.

Regarding soil sample #2: Jesus told us they have **no root in themselves.** In other words, if there had not been so many **rocks** in their lives; in time, they could have understood what they heard. The problem was the rocks, or as I described it, the offenses got in the way. What makes all of this so sad is the fact understanding the Word is what enables us to develop roots. They could have developed roots had they done something about the soil. These people were not forced to be offended. They chose to be offended. It always works this way. **Being offended is a choice.**

> *Great peace have they which love thy law: and nothing shall offend them. (Psalm 119:165)*

Regarding soil sample #3: the problem was even worse. Of this group Jesus used an important phrase: "*he becometh unfruitful.*"

These people had borne fruit. Which means at some point they did understand the Word of the Kingdom. We know this to be true because understanding brings fruit. The existence of the fruit, no matter how temporary confirms there had been a level of understanding. Jesus taught us about the development of fruit when He talked about the fourth group.

However, something very serious happened to the people in soil sample #3. They became **unfruitful. They had understanding but they lost it.**

> *He also that received seed among the thorns is he that heareth the word; and the care of this world, and the deceitfulness of riches, choke the word, and he becometh unfruitful. (Matthew 13:22)*

Those of us who have spent years loving and studying the Word of God view it as a powerful weapon. Frankly, it is hard to comprehend how the care of this world and the deceitfulness of riches could choke the Word out of a person's life. Yet it does. And it seems to happen in such an easy manner. It is the result of a series of choices. **These are rather selfish choices which are in many cases fueled by envy.** We definitely need to talk about this group of people some more.

All three of these groups of people in the parable heard the Word. There is nothing said about anything being wrong with what they heard. It was obviously a pure Word of God. It was not muddled or confusing, but clearly and correctly given to them. In fact, Jesus said the Word was sown in their heart. Jesus did not say there was anything wrong with the **seed** which was sown. The problem was with the **soil.** Jesus did not even tell the disciples what should be done to help them understand. I really do find this part to be amazing.

When I think about this parable and these different types of soil, it brings to my mind the matter of individual responsibility for what happens in our lives. When we hear the Word, we each have a responsibility to make sure we understand what we have heard. If we don't understand then we should do something about it ourselves. **Doing what is necessary to increase our level of understanding is a mark of spiritual maturity.**

These are the instructions the Apostle Paul gave to Timothy.

> *Study to shew thyself approved unto God, a workman that needeth not to be ashamed, rightly dividing the word of truth. (2 Timothy 2:15)*

Paul was specifically speaking to those who divide the Word of Truth. This would of course be the preachers and the teachers of the Gospel. They may be Pastors or Evangelists or fill the role of one of the other ministry gifts Paul listed in his letter to the Church at Ephesus. Whatever the position we must rightly divide the Word of Truth.

According to *Strong's Concordance,* the Greek words for **rightly dividing**[1] mean to make it straight and smooth, to handle aright, to teach the truth directly and correctly. In this context, it can also mean to dissect the Word and expound upon its meaning. This may be a daunting task, but it is essential. It defines the responsibility of every person who teaches and preaches the Word. To not do things this way should make people ashamed.

In his words to Timothy, the Apostle set one of these actions against the other. I will express it like this.

Rightly dividing the Word leads to **not** being **ashamed.**

Not rightly dividing the Word leads to being **ashamed**.

Anyone who stands behind the pulpit should be prepared. Any person who teaches a class should be prepared. Not doing our homework and studying the Word is not acceptable. It is our job to help people understand. What we teach and preach must be clear. Anything less should make a minister ashamed. Teaching or preaching without understanding throws the door wide open for the Devil to bring deception.

There is no other way to explain the words, *does not need to be ashamed.*

As much as I do not want to say it, this is where the church has failed America. Over and over again we have had great opportunities to see God move in miraculous ways in our nation. Millions have flocked to our churches and public meetings. The chance to ensure the future spiritual makeup of America has been put before us several times, just in my lifetime. What happened?

I have witnessed many people in the ministry fall into one of these first three categories of the parable. I find it very sad to say this is especially true of the third group. What stands out is the deceitfulness of riches. This certainly should not be the case but, I know it is true. I have been asking our Father to give us one more chance to get things right, and I believe He will.

This matter of **understanding involves both the sower and the hearer.** This is the point I am making. Actually, I believe the responsibility weighs as much on the sower as it does on the soil.

Here is an intriguing question with regard to this parable. Is the soil totally responsible to make itself into better soil? **Perhaps we have missed it by not taking more time to help people become better soil** before we got them excited about our great revelations. How does soil improve itself? Doesn't soil left unattended become worse and not better? Doesn't erosion occur and wild vegetation grow in unattended soil? How much does good parenting have to do with the development of good soil in children? It has everything to do with it.

Let's look at the parable from another perspective. Isn't it the responsibility of the person who is preaching, teaching, or even just sharing the Word to make sure what they say is easy to understand? **Maybe the real problem has been a lack of understanding on the part of those who were sowing the seed.**

I am fully aware in the parable, Jesus was speaking from the perspective of Him being the sower of the Word. His preparation was full, complete, impeccable and without any flaws. What I am addressing is those who have been called and are attempting to follow in His footsteps. What changes do we need to make?

The Apostle Paul was an excellent communicator.

He did everything he knew how to do to make certain he had done his best at preaching the Gospel. Here is an excellent example in his own words. I chose to use *The Passion Translation* because it is clearer than the *King James Version*.

> *I became "weak" to the weak to win the weak. I have adapted to the culture of every place I've gone so that I could more easily win people to Christ. I've done all this so that I would become God's partner for the sake of the gospel. Isn't it obvious that all runners on the racetrack keep on running to win, but only one receives the victor's prize? Yet each one of you must run the race to be victorious. A true athlete will be disciplined in every respect, practicing constant self-control in order to win a laurel wreath that quickly withers. But we run our race to win a victor's crown that will last forever. For that reason, I don't run just for exercise or box like one throwing aimless punches, but I train like a champion athlete. I subdue my body and get it under my control, so that after preaching the good news to others I myself won't be disqualified. (1 Corinthians 9:22-27 - TPT)*

I fully understand the example is talking about the discipline of our bodies. However, it makes the point regarding our responsibilities to the soil in the Kingdom of Heaven. What we do to win the prize communicates to those in the race with us, something which is either positive or negative.

The word **responsibility** is often treated like it is an ugly, dirty word. It should be obvious to you what not being responsible has done to our world. Not taking responsibility for one's decisions and actions and words is destroying our society.

How did America, the land we love, get to this place? There is no question we can point a finger at failed marriages and broken homes. Children are raising themselves and as could be expected they often do a terrible job. But I am saying some of the blame can be put on the church. This may sound terrible and very condemning unless you understand we must know the real source of the problem in order to work on the right problem.

So, where did the church fail? What happened? What started us down this road? Many put the blame on taking prayer and the Bible out of our schools.

I would agree this has done a lot of damage. I do believe the church could have risen up and stopped it. But the real damage has been done, not so much by what was taken out of our schools, but by **what has been put in** them. I am actually talking about something which began many years ago. Many thought it was so ridiculous it would never be taken seriously. They were certainly wrong.

✕ One of the most damming things done to the minds of children is the teaching of evolution as it was expressed in Charles Darwin's book, *On The Origin of Species*.

I will not accuse Darwin, personally of having some demonic plan to undermine society by teaching his theories. I don't know if he even considered what his theories might do to the minds of people who didn't have a Biblical World View. Actually, I have not found any information to let me know this was ever his concern.

Whatever the original source of the theory of evolution may have been, this non-scientific lie called evolution did not permeate our schools until Darwin's book made it popular. **I call it a lie** because it is passed off as fact, when nothing about it has ever been, or ever will be proven.

I am convinced the real underlying purpose for wanting people to believe in evolution is to **elevate man and demote God.** Certainly, I am not accusing Darwin of this, because I have no evidence. I do not know if this was his motive. I am speaking of the current purpose for using these theories. Darwin may have only thought he had discovered an explanation for the existence of this planet and everything on it. Of course, the theory was fatally flawed because he left God the creator out of the theory.

More than the basic theory I am disturbed by the obvious motives of those who have used Darwin's ideas to promote their own agenda. **This agenda is pagan!** This agenda is **atheistic.** This agenda would completely remove all thoughts and ideas about God from our society if it could. This is the real foundation under many of those who are in places of power in our nation today. Their entire educational experience had evolution as a backdrop.

Before this lie we know of as evolution took hold in our educational system; for the most part we were a Christian nation. We believed God was in control and not man. We believed God made us the way we are both male and female. We did not choose this ourselves. It is now flabbergasting to see the confusion and absolute insistence of some regarding their opinion about how many genders there are. I don't have words to express how ridiculous this sounds.

As a nation we once believed God created the wonders of the universe, this earth and everything on it. At least the majority of the people believed these things. Only God could and would decide when this earth would cease to be. We had a standard against which we measured things to determine what is normal and right.

Evolution has destroyed this standard for people who know nothing about God and his Word. When God was removed as the origin and source of life and everything relating to it, all which was absolute and definite was gone in the minds of our children. If it didn't happen in the public schools in the lower grades it happened to millions of kids in the Colleges and Universities. Some of these were supposed to be Christian Universities. They even have the word "Christian" in their name.

In this pagan and heathenistic manner of thinking man is seen as the source and cause of everything good. Therefore man must also be blamed for everything that is bad. This is most notable when people of this mindset talk about what is happening to our natural resources.

This may sound too simple, but **man simply can't bear the weight of what he has created in his own mind.** The results can be absurd. When men can't own up to their mistakes, they always find something else to blame. One of the greatest examples is the claim we are destroying the planet. We didn't create it, but somehow, we can destroy it. This is how crazy things become when people are completely void of an understanding of the kingdom.

My assessment of the culture we now confront makes it sound like these are recent developments in humanity. Actually, it is a replay of mans perverted Godless thinking which has been around since the beginning of time. I am sure you are familiar with these words. They are not pleasant to read. However, these words, written almost 2000 years ago are very descriptive of our society. It is one void of an understanding heart.

> *For the invisible things of him from the creation of the world are clearly seen, being understood by the things that are made, even his eternal power and Godhead; so that they are without excuse: Because that, when they knew God, they glorified him not as God, neither were thankful; but became vain in their imaginations, and their foolish heart was darkened. Professing themselves to be wise, they became fools, And changed the glory of the uncorruptible God into an image made like to corruptible man, and to birds, and four-footed beasts, and creeping things. Wherefore God also gave them up to uncleanness through the lusts of their own hearts, to dishonor their own bodies between themselves: Who changed the truth of God into a lie, and worshiped and served the creature more than the Creator, who is blessed for ever. Amen. For this cause God gave them up unto vile affections: for even their women did change the natural use into that which is against nature: And likewise also the men, leaving the natural use of the woman, burned in their lust one toward another; men*

with men working that which is unseemly, and receiving in themselves that recompense of their error which was meet. And even as they did not like to retain God in their knowledge, God gave them over to a reprobate mind, to do those things which are not convenient; Being filled with all unrighteousness, fornication, wickedness, covetousness, maliciousness; full of envy, murder, debate, deceit, malignity; whisperers, Backbiters, haters of God, despiteful, proud, boasters, inventors of evil things, disobedient to parents, Without understanding, covenant breakers, without natural affection, implacable, unmerciful: Who knowing the judgment of God, that they which commit such things are worthy of death, not only do the same, but have pleasure in them that do them. (Romans 1:20-32)

Paul finally just says it; "without understanding."

Lest you find this so troubling you can't sleep, let me remind you what Paul described is the culture which existed when the Church began. **This is the kind of world Jesus was born into.** All is not lost. This is the kind of world in which the church began. Look how far the Church and the Gospel has come in spite of these things. Hundreds of thousands of people who were living in this squalor, loved Jesus and made Him Lord of their lives.

We can decide to change our world. We can root this stuff out with the mysteries of the kingdom. This is why Jesus revealed them to us. It is so we can bring change to the hearts of men and women. We can help them have an understanding heart. We know how to do it.

In this liberal way of thinking I have just described; every person has become a law unto themselves. **The very thought of being responsible to a higher power for their decisions and actions appears to be gone.** People with no understanding of the Word of the Kingdom have no desire, or knowledge, or will, to live responsibly before God. It is completely acceptable to be irresponsible in every aspect of life. The examples are too numerous to mention.

The book of Judges records the condition in Israel many years ago. It says this:

> *In those days there was no king in Israel: every man did that which was right in his own eyes. (Judges 21:25)*

This is speaking of a natural king. Things get much worse when Jesus is not King in the lives of the people.

Whether or not I am right about the teaching of evolution; one thing is certain. Something or perhaps many things has caused the King of the ages to be replaced with a very self-centered irresponsible way of thinking in the minds of a rather large group of people in the United States. This scripture vividly describes the results.

> *Woe unto them that call evil good, and good evil; that put darkness for light, and light for darkness; that put bitter for sweet, and sweet for bitter! (Isaiah 5:20)*

How many times have I heard someone say, "I never dreamed I would see things like this happen in my country!" Selling Marijuana is legal. Same sex marriage is legal. Women going topless in public is OK according to the higher courts in several states.

I realize this is a lot of negative discourse. Only because it is necessary to have this context, to fully grasp the difference between the heart of many of the people around you and the understanding heart, have I taken time to say these things. But I want to close this chapter on a positive note.

Change is coming! The situation is not hopeless. Always in the darkest hours of human history God has moved on the scene to deliver His creation. There will only be one time when God does not do this. That will be the end of the age and we will already be gone.

I can say these things to you with great conviction

because I know God has put something in man the Devil can't erase or completely stamp out. It is called the **conscience.** People try in many ways to hide it, drown it out or cover it up. But when the high is gone, when the sober moments come, the conscience is alive and well. Yes, it can be seared beyond being effective. However, I have found this to be rare even in the worst of sinners. Never forget, **the Spirit of God is always working,** especially when the ungodly are alone. Paul spoke about this too.

> *For when the gentiles, who have not the law, do by nature the things contained in the law, they, not having the law, are a law unto themselves, which shows the work of the law written in their hearts, their conscience also bearing witness, and their thoughts between accusing and excusing one another. (Romans 2:14-15 - KJ21)*

My precious wife Donna spoke to a woman not long ago who said she does not go to church. Donna asked her why she does not go and invited her to our church. Her reason for not going to church is because her boyfriend likes to go to the casino and gamble. She told Donna going to church makes him feel condemned. Apparently neither this woman nor her boyfriend understands the source of the condemnation. It is his heart condemning him. I suspect her heart condemns her also. Otherwise she would be in church without him.

Jesus did not come into the world to condemn the world. The condemnation is already in full play. It is raging inside millions of unbelievers, even if they do not know why. All the while the solution is a short distance away.

> For if our heart condemn us, God is greater than our heart, and knoweth all things. Beloved, if our heart condemn us not, then have we confidence toward God. (1 John 3:20-21)

Another wonderful secret of the Kingdom of Heaven has been revealed. **We do not need to live our lives in condemnation.** This is not the will of God for us. We can be very confident in the presence of God. We can be very confident when we talk to Him in prayer. I am sure you noticed this all comes back to the heart. What does your heart understand?

A great change is coming to the United States. No, I do not have a date for when this will happen. I just know it will happen. It has been prophesied many times. Interestingly enough it is already in full swing in other parts of the world. I come back rather frequently to these words from *Isaiah 35:1-10*.

> The wilderness and the solitary place shall be glad for them; and the desert shall rejoice, and blossom as the rose. It shall blossom abundantly,

and rejoice even with joy and singing: the glory of Lebanon shall be given unto it, the excellency of Carmel and Sharon, they shall see the glory of the Lord, and the excellency of our God. Strengthen ye the weak hands, and confirm the feeble knees. Say to them that are of a fearful heart, Be strong, fear not: behold, your God will come with vengeance, even God with a recompense; he will come and save you. Then the eyes of the blind shall be opened, and the ears of the deaf shall be unstopped. Then shall the lame man leap as an hart, and the tongue of the dumb sing: for in the wilderness shall waters break out, and streams in the desert. And the parched ground shall become a pool, and the thirsty land springs of water: in the habitation of dragons, where each lay, shall be grass with reeds and rushes. And an highway shall be there, and a way, and it shall be called The way of holiness; the unclean shall not pass over it; but it shall be for those: the wayfaring men, though fools, shall not err therein. No lion shall be there, nor any ravenous beast shall go up thereon, it shall not be found there; but the redeemed shall walk there: And the ransomed of the Lord shall return, and come to Zion with songs and everlasting joy upon their heads: they shall obtain joy and gladness, and sorrow and sighing shall flee away.

There is no question these verses are talking about Israel. However, because we are people of faith, we have become the seed of Abraham. So, these verses apply equally to us. This prophecy is for our day. The fulfillment has already begun.

In case you wonder how these things can be, I will remind you of these words from the Psalmist.

> *The entrance of thy words giveth light;*
> *it giveth understanding unto the simple.*
> *(Psalm 119:130)*

I will keep doing my job and turning the light on. **The light of the Word of the Kingdom will bring understanding to simple people who do not yet have an understanding heart.** This is another **secret** of the Kingdom of Heaven.

Chapter Eleven

A Thorny Subject

———

We will now examine **the heart condition** of the third group of people Jesus spoke about in this parable. These people live among the **thorns.** Jesus explained their lives in this manner.

> *He also that received seed among the thorns is he that heareth the word; and the care of this world, and the deceitfulness of riches, choke the word, and he becometh unfruitful. (Matthew 13:22)*

Certain key words and phrases leap from the page every time I read this verse. Jesus made it so obvious what these **thorns** are in the lives of these people. They are *the care of this world* and *the deceitfulness of riches.*

These two things have a devastating effect in the life

of a Christian. They **choke** out the Word of the Kingdom which has been sown in their heart. The result is a very sad state. These people living among the **thorns** then become unfruitful.

Many times, I have wondered about this matter of becoming **unfruitful**. The **source** of my wondering was not meditating on this verse, it was from observing people. I am thinking especially of ministers I have known both personally and from some distance. At one time their lives and ministries were very fruitful. I am not determining this by the size of the crowds they drew nor their national acclaim. I am going by the obvious results which were evident in the people to whom they ministered.

Today some of these ministers no longer preach salvation. Some never speak in their Heavenly language and certainly do not encourage others to do so. I had one of these men tell me to my face he is not sure he even believes in divine healing any longer. Another one says there is no Hell and every human will go to Heaven. He has gone so far as to say being born-again is not necessary. **The thorns got to these people.**

God never intended for us to live among the thorns. When God expelled Adam and Eve from the Garden of Eden, He made statements to both of them regarding what they and their descendants would face. It was not pleasant and we still must overcome these things.

And unto Adam he said, Because thou hast hearkened unto the voice of thy wife, and hast eaten of the tree, of which I commanded thee, saying, Thou shalt not eat of it: cursed is the ground for thy sake; in sorrow shalt thou eat of it all the days of thy life; Thorns also and this-tles shall it bring forth to thee; and thou shalt eat the herb of the field; In the sweat of thy face shalt thou eat bread, till thou return unto the ground; for out of it wast thou taken: for dust thou art, and unto dust shalt thou return. (Genesis 3:17-19)

The description we are given of the Garden of Eden causes me to believe God intended only wonderful things for the man and woman He created. They would never be in want. Everything they desired would be abundantly and readily available. To our way of thinking they would live in absolute wealth and splendor. They would never have a care in the world. After-all isn't this the picture we have of eternity with God?

It was the fall of man and the curse which ensued which brought the natural thorns and the spiritual thorns. It was the fall of man and the curse pronounced by God which caused the thorns to grow on this earth. **Never did God intend for man to be consumed by the thorns.** He had a better plan. This plan is only found in the Word of the Kingdom. It is one of its most profound and wonderful secrets. I am speaking of how to live this life free of care with every need supplied. It is a life of watching as your desires are fulfilled as God directs your footsteps. Yet many of God's people get caught in the thorns. They think they can do this better than God by using their own plans. It never works out this way.

Believing that by ourselves we can overcome the curse God put on this earth when Adam fell is a mistake. An example of this is thinking money can solve all our problems. **This is the deceitfulness of riches.** The enemy tries to convince us if we only had enough money, we would **never have a care in the world.** Yet we see ample evidence from the wealthiest of people this certainly does not work. Many wealthy people seem to have the weight of the world on their shoulders. The misery and the suicide rate among this group of people is staggering. Drugs and alcohol consumption plague a great many of them, unless they know Jesus.

These two things, the care of this world and the deceitfulness of riches were most likely a problem **before** these people ever heard the Word. These two things present challenges for all of us. If they are a great problem for us before we hear the Word of the Kingdom, they may remain a problem while we are hearing the Word. This may still be a challenge after we hear the Word **if we don't learn to deal with them.** I have certainly observed this to be so.

Hearing the Word does not cause us to get caught up in the care of the world. Hearing the Word does not cause us to get caught up in the deceitfulness of riches. Learning the mysteries of the Kingdom should enable us to deal with both of these things.

The problem this group of people had when Jesus said these words to His disciples is the same problem we face today. Other voices were speaking into their lives. They made a habit of listening to the wrong things instead of hearing the Word and learning its secrets. Many voices are speaking in our world. **The voices to which we take heed make a great difference in the way things turn out.**

These words from Jesus have great significance for our lives.

> *Then said Jesus to those Jews which believed on him, If ye continue in my word, then are ye my disciples indeed; And ye shall know the truth, and the truth shall make you free. (John 8:31-32)*

There were Jews who believed in Jesus; and we believe in Him. The **seed** has been sown in our hearts. But according to what Jesus told these Jews, just hearing the Word of the Kingdom is not enough. Just knowing about the **mysteries** of the kingdom is not enough. We must continue in the Word.

To continue in the Word means: **to hear more of the Word and to do something with what we hear.** We must put the Word into practice in our lives. We must know about the Word of the Kingdom and the secrets we find in it. Then these mysteries must become a functional part of daily living. Live like you are a part of this kingdom. Speak and act like you are a part of this kingdom. Why? Because we are citizens of this kingdom.

It has been my distinct privilege to travel to numerous countries of the world. I quickly discovered something different about each of them. Even in the English-speaking countries where we shared a common language, many of the words had very different meanings. The food was different. The houses were different. I also realized these **Kingdoms** (or countries) to use this word loosely were not just different for the sake of being different. The **words** of each of these Kingdoms had made them different. Those words had a profound impact on what the people believed about themselves. It dictated to them the manner in which they should live and act.

My most interesting discovery in my travels was what I experienced in the churches. I was traveling in Germany and was invited to speak in a local German church. This was the only time I spoke in a church with different doctrine to what I embrace from the Word of God. This was a very formal German church, deeply entrenched in their religion. I preached a very clear salvation message.

The people and the minister in this German church were very respectful and listened intently. This was the first time an American preacher had ever spoken in their church. This may have also been the first clear message they had heard on how to be saved.

The other churches and meetings where I ministered were of the same faith and belief as I have. In some they spoke a different language. In some where the English language was the predominant language, even then I found it necessary to explain many of the things I said to them. However, one thing stood out to me above all else in these church meetings.

When it came time to worship God, suddenly I knew we were a part of the same kingdom. It was a kingdom which transcended our natural differences. **It was the Kingdom of Heaven in demonstration in all of these different countries.** We all had different levels of understanding of the Word of the Kingdom and its secrets. Nevertheless, we knew we were citizens of the same kingdom.

This brings me to another important part of the passage in John chapter 8 where Jesus went on to speak of continuing in the Word. Disciples are not just hearers of the Word. They are also doers of the Word. This is where discipleship actually begins. **We start doing the things we have heard and this moves us to the next level.** We no longer just know about the truth. We are living it!

Hearing alone does not result in knowing. Too many people think it does. The results of this thinking have been disastrous.

You don't know the Word until you understand the Word. **You don't know the truth until you understand the truth.** This is what continuing in the Word will do for you. It will give you understanding of the truth. It is understanding the truth that makes you free. The proof of what I am saying is the difference we see in people who are free and people who are not free. The people who are not free are still entangled in the **thorns** their lives were caught in before they heard the Word. This entanglement is the result of not continuing in the Word. By continuing in the Word, I am expressing the fact we must be doers of the Word. We must take what we have heard and apply it to our lives. It is in the application of the Word where we discover the necessary changes. **Therefore, the thorns are really the result of never developing an understanding heart and making the necessary changes.**

We all know people we love who have heard the Word. Instead of doing what they heard they reverted right back to their old way of thinking. Their days and nights are consumed with going back and forth between what the Word says and what their mind says. This is a miserable way to live. It is an accurate description of **being caught in the thorns.** It is a painful struggle with the cares of this world and the deceitfulness of riches.

The Apostle Paul addressed this issue as follows.

But what things were gain to me, those I counted loss for Christ. Yea doubtless, and I count all things but loss for the excellency of the knowledge of Christ Jesus my Lord: for whom I have suffered the loss of all things, and do count them but dung, that I may win Christ, And be found in him, not having mine own righteousness, which is of the law, but that which is through the faith of Christ, the righteousness which is of God by faith: That I may know him, and the power of his resurrection, and the fellowship of his sufferings, being made conformable unto his death; If by any means I might attain unto the resurrection of the dead. Not as though I had already attained, either were already perfect: but I follow after, if that I may apprehend that for which also I am apprehended of Christ Jesus. Brethren, I count not myself to have apprehended: but this one thing I do, forgetting those things which are behind, and reaching forth unto those things which are before, I press toward the mark for the prize of the high calling of God in Christ Jesus. (Philippians 3:7-14)

Those words define the life of the Apostle Paul. In verse ten the Greek word **ginosko**[1] is translated as **know**.

We have the same Greek word used by Jesus when He said: *"you shall know the truth."* In both cases the word **ginosko** could have been translated **understand**. We need to understand the truth. This is key to developing an understanding heart. The verse in Philippians 3:10 could also read: *That I may understand him, and (understand) the power of his resurrection, and (understand) the fellowship of his sufferings, being made conformable unto his death.*

I am confident the translators were careful not to use the word understand because they probably did not believe it was possible to understand any of these things mentioned. Yet, these are mysteries of the kingdom our Father wants us to know. He wants us to understand.

Here is another secret of the kingdom revealed in these verses from the book of Philippians. **It is the single-mindedness which is necessary to get away from the thorns.** Paul used these words, *"this one thing I do."* If you have ever been caught in a blackberry bush or even a rose bush then you know you can't be thinking and doing other things while you are trying to get untangled. Getting free from those thorns is the only thing you care about doing.

As a young boy, growing up in Arkansas, I have had lots of experience with blackberry vines. My family loved blackberries and all the wonderful things you can make with them, especially blackberry cobbler. When

I was a young child we did not go to the grocery store and buy blackberries in the frozen food section. So, each year my parents were excited as they anticipated the time when the blackberries were ripe and ready to pick. We lived just a few miles from an old deserted property where there were lots of blackberry vines.

Sometimes on a Saturday morning, my parents would wake my sister and me before sunrise to go pick blackberries. Our parents always told us to dress so every inch of skin except for our faces was covered to protect us from the hot sun. When we got to the blackberry patch we discovered the real reason for these instructions.

We waded out into the blackberry patch to discover this was not a simple, easy task. There were chiggers. If you do not know what that little bug is you are very fortunate. You can barely see them. They live in the grass and are just waiting to get on you and bite you. The itching is worse than anything a mosquito could ever cause. Of course there were mosquitoes too. There were bees and wasps and other things we really did not want to be around. But the worst part was the stickers on the vines. They just called them little prickles, but to a young boy, these were thorns.

These stickers are all over the stems of the vines. They may be small thorns, but they can do a lot of damage to your skin. In spite of all the clothing and the gloves we wore, we always came home with lots of scratches.

Picking blackberries is a lot of work. There were a lot of berries, but it was hard to get to them because of all the stickers. To a little kid these plants looked like something fighting itself. The same vine that produced the stickers also produced the blackberries. It almost looked as though the vine was trying to overcome or choke out the fruit. Of course my parents explained the thorns were there to protect the blackberries.

This is what I think of when I read what Jesus said about the thorns choking out the Word of the Kingdom. For a while the fruit is there with the thorns. Eventually there is nothing left but the thorns. Even if we did not pick the blackberries or the birds did not eat them, they would spoil and fall off the vines. There was nothing left but the thorny vines. When all the leaves were gone the thorns remained.

This is the way it works when people are caught up in the cares of this world and the deceitfulness of riches. It may look good for a while. They still benefit from the fruit for a short time, but eventually this changes. They are left with nothing but the thorns.

As I stated earlier, Jesus described these **thorns** in two ways. One type of thorn is the care of this world. The other type of thorn is the deceitfulness of riches. What did Jesus mean by the care of this world? Read this next passage carefully and thoughtfully and I believe you will understand what Jesus was teaching.

Therefore I say unto you, Take no thought for your life, what ye shall eat, or what ye shall drink; nor yet for your body, what ye shall put on. Is not the life more than meat, and the body than raiment? Behold the fowls of the air: for they sow not, neither do they reap, nor gather into barns; yet your Heavenly Father feedeth them. Are ye not much better than they? Which of you by taking thought can add one cubit unto his stature? And why take ye thought for raiment? Consider the lilies of the field, how they grow; they toil not, neither do they spin: And yet I say unto you, That even Solomon in all his glory was not arrayed like one of these. Wherefore, if God so clothe the grass of the field, which to day is, and to morrow is cast into the oven, shall he not much more clothe you, O ye of little faith? Therefore take no thought, saying, What shall we eat? or, What shall we drink? or, Wherewithal shall we be clothed? (For after all these things do the Gentiles seek:) for your Heavenly Father knoweth that ye have need of all these things. But seek ye first the Kingdom of God, and his righteousness; and all these things shall be added unto you. Take therefore no thought for the morrow: for the morrow shall take thought for the things of itself. Sufficient unto the day is the evil thereof. (Matthew 6:25-34)

Jesus was not telling us we don't need food and clothing. Neither was He saying we can be lazy and do nothing and all of this will just come to us. The issue here is worrying about these things and being filled with anxiety about everything in our lives. The challenge is to add faith to what we do on a regular basis to just live. I can't change tomorrow and neither can you. But I can face the future with great faith in a great God!

> *Be anxious for nothing, but in everything by prayer and supplication, with thanksgiving, let your requests be made known to God; and the peace of God, which surpasses all understanding. (Philippians 4:6-7 - NKJV)*

That is how you deal with the cares of this world. Our natural understanding will always fail us when we think about the future. The concerns about climate change are a good example. Sometimes I laugh at how ridiculous the suggestions are. The things this crowd believes are absurd. It really is not funny when we realize this crazy stuff is being taught in our schools and universities. It never seems to register how much they have been wrong and how often their reasoning has failed them. They worry about things they can never change.

Some people have so much money they worry about it? Some people have so little money they worry about it. Money should never create anxiety in your life.

You can have great plans for your future and even have figured out how you think it will all happen and you can still worry about it. You can be in a place where you have no idea what the future holds and you can worry about that too.

Why worry? It never accomplishes anything good!

> *Humble yourselves therefore under the mighty hand of God, that he may exalt you in due time: Casting all your care upon him; for he careth for you. Be sober, be vigilant; because your adversary the devil, as a roaring lion, walketh about, seeking whom he may devour: Whom resist steadfast in the faith, knowing that the same afflictions are accomplished in your brethren that are in the world. (1 Peter 5:6-9)*

Our family did not have much when I was a child. Neither of my parents finished school and good paying jobs were not available to them. Other people suffer in much worse poverty than we did. Nonetheless it was not pleasant from a financial standpoint. I had wonderful parents who loved me and they loved God without question. For this Spiritual heritage I am very grateful. But nothing from the things they talked about at my church taught me how to trust in God for what I needed. By the grace and mercy of God I discovered these things on my own.

Granted it was not easy. It was not without considerable difficulty. Many times, I cried out to God wondering how things would turn out for me. It probably was more stubbornness than anything else but I made a decision not to worry. This was a battle and I did not know why it was so hard. To be really honest, **it felt better not to worry than it did to worry.** If you had asked me why at the time, I could not have given you an answer. Once I understood in my heart God would take care of me if I would trust him and obey Him, I stopped worrying. The struggle ended because I understood God was on my side. I continue to live this way to this day. What I just told you happened when I was very young.

Getting rid of thorns is not easy. This is true of the natural kind of thorns and the spiritual kind of thorns. It takes making decisions and staying with them. Here is a story about some very close friends of Jesus.

> *Now it came to pass, as they went, that he entered into a certain village: and a certain woman named Martha received him into her house. And she had a sister called Mary, which also sat at Jesus' feet, and heard his word. But Martha was cumbered (driven about mentally, distracted, over-occupied and too busy) about much serving, and came to him, and said, Lord, dost thou not care that my sister hath left me to serve alone? bid her therefore*

that she help me. And Jesus answered and said unto her, Martha, Martha, thou art careful and troubled about many things: But one thing is needful: and Mary hath chosen that good part, which shall not be taken away from her. (Luke 10:38-42)

There were actually four people involved in this story. The one not mentioned is the brother we know by the name of Lazarus, whom Jesus raised from the dead. All four of them had to eat. Food was necessary and I am certain Jesus appreciated all Martha did for him. But Jesus did not want Martha to be so wrapped up in the things she was doing for Him that she missed out on what He could do for her.

Never allow yourself to get so wrapped up in what you can do for Jesus you miss out on what Jesus can do for you. Don't get so wrapped up in what you can do for yourself you miss out on what Jesus can do for you. This is the way these **thorns** begin to take root and grow in a person's life.

When we looked at the verses in Matthew 13 did you notice Jesus did not say the cares of this world and riches are evil or bad. It is the **deceitfulness** of these things which is a problem. What Jesus was addressing was how we deal with this deceitfulness. For a better understanding, let's look at the deceitfulness of riches.

Then one from the crowd said to Him, "Teacher, tell my brother to divide the inheritance with me." But He said to him, "Man, who made Me a judge or an arbitrator over you?" And He said to them, "Take heed and beware of covetousness, for one's life does not consist in the abundance of the things he possesses." Then He spoke a parable to them, saying: "The ground of a certain rich man yielded plentifully. And he thought within himself, saying, 'What shall I do, since I have no room to store my crops?' So he said, 'I will do this: I will pull down my barns and build greater, and there I will store all my crops and my goods. And I will say to my soul, "Soul, you have many goods laid up for many years; take your ease; eat, drink, and be merry."' But God said to him, 'Fool! This night your soul will be required of you; then whose will those things be which you have provided?' "So is he who lays up treasure for himself, and is not rich toward God." (Luke 12:13-21 - NKJV)

There are two statements in those verses which say it so well. *One's life does not consist in the abundance of the things he possesses.* **When a person lives like their life is all about what they possess this is the deceitfulness of riches.** The evidence is often seen in the stingy or haughty attitude of these people. But here is another clue.

He who lays up treasure for himself, and is not rich toward God... The issue in this story Jesus told is not one of preparing or not preparing for our future. We should all handle our finances in a responsible manner so we are not dependent on society to take care of us when we can no longer work. However, we must never just prepare for our future and not be rich toward God.

When Jesus said: *"rich toward God"* Jesus was talking about tithing and giving. When some people teach on tithing and giving, they miss the underlying purpose for doing it. **Every time we tithe and give we are making it clear where our trust lies.** We are saying to the father my trust is not in money or my ability to make money. My confidence is not in having a lot of money. My trust is in you. The story of the rich young ruler comes to mind.

> *Now behold, one came and said to Him, "Good Teacher, what good thing shall I do that I may have eternal life?" So He said to him, "Why do you call Me good? No one is good but One, that is, God. But if you want to enter into life, keep the commandments." He said to Him, "Which ones?" Jesus said, "'You shall not murder,' 'You shall not commit adultery,' 'You shall not steal,' 'You shall not bear false witness,' 'Honor your father and your mother,' and, 'You shall love your neighbor as yourself.'" The young man said to Him,*

"All these things I have kept from my youth. What do I still lack?" Jesus said to him, "If you want to be perfect, go, sell what you have and give to the poor, and you will have treasure in Heaven; and come, follow Me." But when the young man heard that saying, he went away sorrowful, for he had great possessions. (Matthew 19:16-22 - NKJV)

The response Jesus gave this young rich man was not that he should live in poverty in order to have eternal life. No amount of money and no amount of poverty will give you eternal life. Only faith in God gives us eternal life. **Eternal life has nothing to do with money.**

Consider with me for a moment what Jesus said to this young man about giving to the poor. Think about the notion some have regarding this conversation. Apparently, some people do believe poverty has something to do with pleasing God and eternal life. So, pretend with me for a moment the rich man gave all his money to the poor. If the rich young ruler gave what he had to the poor they would no longer be poor. Doesn't this mean if they kept what the rich man gave them, they would not have eternal life? If having money kept the rich young ruler from having eternal life, the same would be true for these poor people once they got money.

Jesus was not just talking to this rich young man

about how much money he had. This was not the real problem. Jesus wanted him to understand the deceitfulness of riches. He was endeavoring to teach the young man about being rich toward God.

Having a lot of money convinces some people they are secure and their future is guaranteed. Some come to believe because they have lots of money they are smarter than other people, thus they should have more power. They should be treated better than others because they are more important. **This is the deceitfulness of riches.** These are **thorns** and they **choke** out the Word.

The Word of God teaches us to be kind and loving and generous. We are not to be selfish. We are told not to think more highly of ourselves than we ought to think. It is easy to see how these things from the Word are counter to the thinking of those who are deceived by wealth.

The use of the word **choke** is interesting. Another word for choke is to **suffocate.** These things mentioned in the parable suffocate the Word.

Choking can be a rather slow way to die. I know there are ways for it to be speed-ed up, but I am thinking more of accidental choking. There is a reason Jesus used the word **choke.** People with this kind of soil may experience the loss of the Word which produces fruit in their lives very slowly.

The thorns of life continually cause them to worry. Or, they get so deceived by the riches, which can happen over time, they convince themselves they are in control.

There is one more general observation I have about Matthew 13:19-21; before I talk about the fourth and final group of people in this parable.

According to verse 19 - the Word was taken away from these people almost immediately.

According to verse 21 - the words *dureth for a while* indicate the people in this second group kept the Word in their lives a little longer than the first group.

But according to verse 22 - **the thorns take even longer to choke out the Word.** Consider how a wild thorn bush takes over part of a fence line or a field. It is a slow but steady process. This is the picture Jesus wanted us to have. **Eventually the thorns will push the Word out.**

> *The thief cometh not, but for to steal, and to kill, and to destroy: I am come that they might have life, and that they might have it more abundantly." (John 10:10)*

We have often talked about the Devil stealing things from people. And he most definitely does what he is here to do. Yet I dare to say what he wants most to steal from us is the Word which has been sown in our hearts. He does not want us to ever understand it and benefit from the fruit it can produce in our lives.

Jesus told His disciples three ways the Devil attacks. We can benefit greatly from understanding these things. However, I am determined to be a part of this last group of people and do my best to help you be a part of this fruit-bearing group. I intend to be one of those who brings forth one hundred-fold.

Here is a wonderful story about a dream which Solomon had. He had just become the king and felt very inadequate to do the job. We have a record of this amazing conversation Solomon had with God. This will be helpful to us as we examine what Jesus said to the group of people He declared to be good soil.

> *And Solomon loved the Lord, walking in the statutes of David his father: only he sacrificed and burnt incense in high places. And the king went to Gibeon to sacrifice there; for that was the great high place: a thousand burnt offerings did Solomon offer upon that altar. In Gibeon the Lord appeared to Solomon in a dream by night: and God said, Ask what I shall give thee. And Solomon said, Thou hast shewed unto thy servant David my father great mercy, according as he walked before thee in*

truth, and in righteousness, and in uprightness of heart with thee; and thou hast kept for him this great kindness, that thou hast given him a son to sit on his throne, as it is this day. And now, O Lord my God, thou hast made thy servant king instead of David my father: and I am but a little child: I know not how to go out or come in. And thy servant is in the midst of thy people which thou hast chosen, a great people, that cannot be numbered nor counted for multitude. Give therefore thy servant an understanding heart to judge thy people, that I may discern between good and bad: for who is able to judge this thy so great a people? (1 Kings 3:3-9)

Chapter Twelve

A Big-hearted Person

———

As we begin our study of the fourth group of people Jesus spoke about in the parable of the sower let's take a further look at the conversation between God and Solomon.

In his dream God said to Solomon: "Ask what I shall give thee." (1 Kings 3:5)

After making several statements Solomon replied: "Give therefore thy servant an understanding heart to judge thy people, that I may discern between good and bad: for who is able to judge this thy so great a people"? (1 Kings 3:9)

The first thing which stands out to me in the request of Solomon is the lack of selfishness. At this point in his life Solomon had not become a self-centered person. **You cannot have an understanding heart as long as you think of yourself as the center of your universe.** The request Solomon made to God was based on his desire to help the people over whom he had been made king.

This is the response God made to Solomon's request.

> *"And God gave Solomon wisdom and understanding exceeding much, and largeness of heart, even as the sand that is on the sea shore." (1 Kings 4:29)*

There is an interesting mixture of words in those verses. These are the three combinations of words which really stand out to me. Solomon asked for an understanding heart. In response God gave Solomon **wisdom**. Then God gave him **understanding exceedingly much**. To this God added **largeness of heart**. I really believe this is a process which occurs in the development of an understanding heart. I also believe it happens in this specific order.

This is not as complicated as it might appear. No one would ask for an understanding heart unless they first had some wisdom. **Asking for an understanding heart is indicative of wisdom.** But more wisdom is available. At the same time wisdom, understanding exceedingly much, and largeness of heart are the results of having an understanding heart. Let's look at each of these.

The first word is **wisdom**. This is a huge subject and frankly not one which is well understood. Some have reduced the meaning of wisdom to simply knowing how to use the knowledge we have received. It is much more than this.

Solomon penned these words in what we know as the Book of Proverbs.

> *Get wisdom, get understanding: forget it not; neither decline from the words of my mouth. Forsake her not, and she shall preserve thee: love her, and she shall keep thee. Wisdom is the principal thing; therefore get wisdom: and with all thy getting get understanding. Exalt her, and she shall promote thee: she shall bring thee to honour, when thou dost embrace her. She shall give to thine head an ornament of grace: a crown of glory shall she deliver to thee. (Proverbs 4:5-9)*

I have heard this passage used in sermons and all of the focus was placed on wisdom. It is easy to see why this happens. Solomon said: *"Wisdom is the principal thing; therefore get wisdom."* It only makes sense to conclude everything else Solomon said is tied to this wisdom. But what if it isn't? What if we take another look at these Scriptures and examine other possibilities? Solomon did add: *"and with all thy getting get understanding."*

Might I suggest what we are really in need of is understanding? How about: wisdom and understanding exceedingly much, and largeness of heart? In other words, I am asking, have we made a mistake in only considering what Solomon said about wisdom?

Here is another question. Wisdom is the principal thing. What did Solomon mean by the **principal thing?**[1]

According to the *Strong's Concordance* it could be the first thing or the best thing or the chief or most important thing. **I am suggesting we consider wisdom to be the place where we begin.** I am also suggesting understanding is essential to the proper use of wisdom.

The Complete Jewish Bible says: *"The beginning of wisdom is: get wisdom!"* *"And along with all your getting, get insight!"*

I take this to mean only a wise person will seek wisdom. The first step to having wisdom is to make it a priority in your life. Very few people seem to ever do this.

The Easy To Read Version of the Bible says: *"The first step to becoming wise is to look for wisdom."*

These translators have the same view of these statements I have. Wisdom is the place where we must begin. Not doing so can lead to serious error.

Going back to *The Complete Jewish Bible* we find the next thing their text says is to *get insight*. **This is a very good definition of understanding.** It is my insight into a particular matter which enables me to make use of the wisdom I have to deal with it.

Combining the words of both these translations tells us some very important things.

Wisdom alone is not sufficient. Wisdom is not insight. **Having understanding is not the same as having wisdom.** Wisdom is not the same as understanding. We must have both of these. God knew it. When Solomon asked for an understanding heart God responded by giving him three things. The first two were wisdom and understanding. We should conclude wisdom and understanding must never be separated. Wisdom and understanding are very different in their scope and purpose. One compliments the other.

Then God made an exciting and very enlightening statement to Solomon. God told Solomon; I am going to give you *"largeness of heart."* What does this mean? The Hebrew word for **largeness**[2] means expanse or width and breadth.

We can conclude God was saying to Solomon; I am going to give you a bigger heart. Of course, this is not talking about his natural heart. A larger physical heart is an indication of something seriously wrong with the heart. God was doing something good to Solomon. He was making Solomon into **a big-hearted person.**

Everyone loves to encounter people who are very big-hearted. What we typically mean by this is they are kind and generous to everyone. They go out of their way to help people. Those who really have wisdom and understanding are this way. But then we must consider the whole phrase: *largeness of heart.*

The Hebrew word translated **heart**[3] can refer to the inner man, the mind, the will, the understanding and of course can be translated heart as the *King James* translators have done. This is all according to the *Strong's Concordance.* Let's consider what this means.

When God promised to give Solomon largeness of heart, he was making a wonderful promise. A change was going to come to his inner man. We often refer to this as the human spirit. Solomon experienced a major change in his spirit. In addition, his mind and his will were changed. Yes, God can change a person's will if they ask Him to do it. Believe me when I tell you this is life changing. Major changes occurred in Solomon as a result of his prayer in this dream.

Solomon's generosity was not just an act or a political move. The elaborate Temple Solomon built is one outstanding example of his generosity. The building of the Temple came before the building of the King's palace. The amazing activity which surrounded the dedication of the Temple and included all of the people of Israel is almost mind-boggling in its extravagance. There are signs of great generosity in his many treaties with the nations around him which created 40 years of peaceful reign.

We often comment on the wisdom of Solomon, and it was great. We can also see a man with a great mind in all of his dealings and the things he built.

It all was the result of wisdom and understanding.

When you develop an understanding heart this effectively causes your heart to be enlarged. This is a very interesting thought isn't it? Your understanding exceeds anything it may have been previously. **An understanding heart changes you; the real you.** I am talking about the spirit man.

Jesus confirms what I have been saying about Solomon in these words.

> *But he that received seed into the good ground is he that heareth the word, and understandeth it; which also beareth fruit, and bringeth forth, some an hundredfold, some sixty, some thirty. (Matthew 13:23)*

I have been using words such as generosity and big-hearted. Jesus used the words *beareth fruit*. Then He quantified this fruit in terms of *an hundredfold, some sixty, some thirty.*

Various interpretations have been applied to the meaning of these statements by Jesus. One thing I am certain is intended by the Lord. **There is definitely a reward for the understanding heart.** The first place I would expect to find this reward would be **the opposite** of what Jesus said in the following statements.

> *For this people's heart is waxed gross, and their ears are dull of hearing, and their eyes they have closed; lest at any time they should see with their eyes and hear with their ears, and should understand with their heart, and should be converted, and I should heal them. (Matthew 13:15-16)*

Follow this logically. If Jesus taught in parables so the people **would not understand** the mysteries of the Kingdom of Heaven, wouldn't an **understanding heart** result in the **opposite?** This is what Jesus told the disciples He was doing. What provoked Jesus to do this was the condition of the ears, eyes and hearts of these people. If what Jesus wanted to prevent was the conversion and healing of these people, then wouldn't an understanding heart result in the opposite of all of this? Let me state this in a positive manner.

⅄ An understanding heart will result in the ears hearing better. The eyes will see better. The heart will enlarge. Conversion and healing will occur.

When *Strong* defined **converted**[4] he said it means to worship the true God; to cause a person to return, to bring back the love and obedience to God, and to love wisdom and righteousness.

The crowd Jesus was speaking to when he made these statements were in no condition to do any of these things. Jesus knew it. However He went on to say this to His disciples. *"But blessed are your eyes, for they see: and your ears, for they hear."*

As wonderful as this statement is, **something is missing.** Jesus did not say at this moment His disciples understood. He did not say this because an understanding of the mysteries of the Kingdom of Heaven had not yet come to them. He had just begun to expose them to these secrets. But he congratulated them on their eyes and ears being open to receive.

I would like to posit this interpretation of the *"hundredfold, some sixty, some thirty"* declaration made by Jesus. No two people experience spiritual growth and development at the same rate. Some grow faster, some grow more slowly. It all depends on the level of their individual understanding.

I am suggesting Jesus was really expressing different levels of an understanding heart. I would go so far as to say what God promised to Solomon did not happen all at once. The promises of God rarely are fulfilled in an instant. Virtually all of them take time to develop.

I will restate this in the words I borrowed from the *Strong's Concordance*[5].

- Our worship of God increases and improves over time.
- Love and obedience to God comes through a growth process.
- Certainly, a love of wisdom and righteousness does not come suddenly.

All of these can be considered as fruit. All of them can be seen at varying levels in the inhabitants of the Kingdom of God.

We do not have a copy of the original manuscript of the things Jesus said. We are left to trust the scribes and the translators. We can only assume Jesus stated this in a descending order as an hundredfold, some sixty, some thirty. But to add a little more insight to the statement let's turn it around for a moment.

What if we start with the thirty and build up to the hundredfold? This would indicate something wonderful is happening as a person's understanding heart develops. It is actually more in line with the typical growth process.

I think everybody would like to be a part of this 4th group. They would be willing to participate at any level. My assumption is based on the fact **the fruit is proof** these people have the Word of the Kingdom working for them.

What is also interesting is **the results are not the same for everybody.** Some ministers have told us we all start out in our relationship with God with the exact same measure of faith. This conclusion is based on a particular interpretation of the following verse of Scripture.

> *For I say, through the grace given unto me, to every man that is among you, not to think of himself more highly than he ought to think; but to think soberly, according as God hath dealt to every man the measure of faith. (Romans 12:3)*

Let's assume this is a correct understanding of this verse. What Jesus said to the disciples in this parable is still true. **The Word sown in people's hearts does not produce the same results in every person.** We begin at the same level with the same measure of faith. However, we don't all achieve the same results. For some it is *an hundredfold, some sixty, some thirty.*

What makes the difference is understanding. Perhaps I should say, a lack of understanding makes the difference. I know someone will read this and think the difference is determined by whether or not people do what they hear from the Word.

Absolutely this will make a difference. However, it raises another important question. Why are some so eager to do the Word they hear and some are not so eager?

Once again this brings us back to the understanding heart. This is the major point of this parable.

Chapter Thirteen

First Comes The Light

———

Every honest person who prays for the sick will admit some people receive their healing and some people don't. Many reasons have been given for this difference.

I am not suggesting healing is only available for certain people. I am not disagreeing with what the Word of God says. I am making reference to the many people who had the same pain, the same sickness or the same disease after they were prayed for. Many of them have died sick. We will never begin to understand why this happens until we confront the reality we face. Yes, I do know what Peter wrote on the subject of healing.

> *Who his own self bare our sins in his own body on the tree, that we, being dead to sins, should live unto righteousness: by whose stripes ye were healed. (1 Peter 2:24)*

In the heart and mind, and in the plan of God we are already healed. No one believes this more than I do.

We have many ways to explain why people do not get healed when we pray for the sick. I am not being sarcastic or critical. I simply am determined to see more results. I want to see them all get healed. My understanding heart is reaching for more and for better answers. Jesus got them all healed in his meetings again and again. Why don't we have the same results?

Undeniably in this parable we are examining, **Jesus made a connection between healing people and them having understanding.** Jesus was talking about them understanding the secrets of the Kingdom of Heaven. He was also talking about their willingness to understand. He was talking about their desire to understand.

Could it be Jesus was telling the disciples; if they have no interest in my kingdom, I have no interest in healing them? My that sounds so harsh. Could a loving Jesus actually think and speak this way? The only way to correctly answer these questions is to consider who was in the crowd.

In Matthew chapter 13, Jesus appears to be addressing some of the same group of people He had spoken to previously. I am basing this on the manner in which chapter 13 begins.

The same day went Jesus out of the house, and sat by the sea side. And great multitudes were gathered together unto him, so that he went into a ship, and sat; and the whole multitude stood on the shore. (Matthew 13:1-2)

Jesus came out of the house where He was staying and as He was sitting by the sea side a large crowd gathered. We can conclude from this; Jesus was in the same location where He had taught previously. Even if the crowd size had increased, Jesus would have easily recognized some of the same people. Jesus had uttered these words.

O generation of vipers, how can ye, being evil, speak good things? for out of the abundance of the heart the mouth speaketh. (Matthew 12:34)

Jesus knew what was in their hearts. I am building up to the point of saying; **what is in your heart can keep you from receiving your healing.** Every person speaks out of what is in their heart on a regular basis. Think about it!

Yes, Jesus did heal many people we would consider to be unsaved. God heals sinners today. But never forget this story.

And, behold, a woman of Canaan came out of the same coasts, and cried unto him, saying,

Have mercy on me, O Lord, thou son of David; my daughter is grievously vexed with a devil. But he answered her not a word. And his disciples came and besought him, saying, Send her away; for she crieth after us. But he answered and said, I am not sent but unto the lost sheep of the house of Israel. Then came she and worshiped him, saying, Lord, help me. But he answered and said, It is not meet to take the children's bread, and to cast it to dogs. And she said, Truth, Lord: yet the dogs eat of the crumbs which fall from their masters' table. Then Jesus answered and said unto her, O woman, great is thy faith: be it unto thee even as thou wilt. And her daughter was made whole from that very hour. (Matthew 15:22-28)

Jesus knew His mission and His purpose in being on this earth. He was very bold to say it. *"I am not sent but unto the lost sheep of the house of Israel."* Jesus was talking about His ministry while He walked this earth. Jesus came to die for the sins of the whole world. However, while He was here He came to the lost sheep of the house of Israel. He came as a **witness to them** and as a **witness against them, if they rejected Him.** This had to be accomplished prior to the Gospel being given to the Gentiles.

Jesus was very bold in the numerous statements He made regarding this matter of why He came to earth.

This story brings me back to my questions. Could it be Jesus was telling the disciples; if they have no interest in my kingdom, I have no interest in healing them? Could a loving Jesus actually think and speak this way?

Until Jesus found out what was in this woman's heart Jesus certainly talked to her this way. He treated her very roughly until He saw her worship Him and speak words of faith out of her mouth. Jesus found in this woman an understanding heart full of faith in Him and what He could do for her daughter. Jesus responded with healing power when she spoke out of what was in her heart.

Jesus is building a kingdom. He is doing it now on this earth. We have come to know it as The Kingdom of God. In what we call The Lord's Prayer Jesus asked for the The Kingdom of Heaven to come to this earth. **Therefore both kingdoms function in exactly the same manner.** They both are based on the Word of the Kingdom which is filled with great mysteries. We need to know these secrets to succeed on this earth.

Now don't let my use of the term, The Kingdom of God confuse you. I have been carefully detailing the Kingdom of Heaven so I could tell you this. God's plan is to mirror or duplicate the Kingdom of Heaven on this earth. This makes it essential to understand the Kingdom of Heaven. Only by doing so can we do our part in The Kingdom of God on this earth.

The ultimate plan is for The Kingdom of God which has been growing and developing on this earth to be merged into the Eternal Kingdom which is The Kingdom of Heaven where our Father resides.

I have repeatedly used the phrase The Kingdom of Heaven with little mention of The Kingdom of God, in order to not confuse the two kingdoms in your mind. Some think these are just two names for the same thing. However, at the present time one is on this earth and one is in Heaven. Once we grasp this we can better understand the interaction between the two.

When God **heals a sinner**, it should **prepare the way for them to be saved** and to enter the Kingdom of Heaven. Of course, from what I just shared with you, they are to be a part of the Kingdom of God on this earth. **By this method we all take the first steps into God's world.** This is all about preparing us for eternity in the Kingdom of Heaven. God's plan is for this to be the start of a growing understanding of the Word of God. This is how we learn all about the Kingdom of Heaven.

When God heals a **Christian**, it should be the result of their understanding of **what rightly belongs to them as a citizen.** They are a child of God. They are simply receiving the children's bread. Never approach your healing acting, thinking or talking like your Father may have run out of bread!

What I am sharing with you is a real mixture of concepts. Some of the more common words and phrases are; faith, understanding, hearing the Word, doing the Word and the renewing of the mind.

One of the major things I am endeavoring to help you see, is when it comes to healing, a lack of understanding the Word is often the real culprit. Faith and understanding are not the same thing.

I have shared with you one of the major important meanings of the Greek word for **understanding** is to set or join together in the mind.[1]

From this definition it is easy to see faith and understanding are not the same thing. Understanding is about **comprehension.** Faith is about **confidence. Understanding** has more to do with your **renewed mind. Faith** has more to do with your **spirit.**

Understanding is what enables you to **keep getting the same results over and over again** when you use your faith. In fact, the areas of your life where your faith is working the best are those areas where you have the greatest and best understanding of the Word, because of your renewed mind.

One major difference in faith and understanding is found in how we receive each of these.

So then faith cometh by hearing, and hearing
by the word of God. (Romans 10:17)

Understanding or comprehension requires much more than just hearing the Word. It requires meditating on what you have heard. It requires thinking about it and finding ways to use what you have heard. In terms of the way our school system used to do things, it requires homework; sometimes lots of it.

Reading is the first key to learning. The second key is comprehending what you are reading. Only when you comprehend can you use what you read.

When school functions the way it should, a lot of time and energy is expended by the teachers and the students working on comprehension. Sadly, we have not done much of this in the church. This is the very core of the problem with regard to healing, finances and especially spiritual growth.

Just hearing the word alone will bring faith to you.
It will not necessarily bring comprehension.

Faith comes to you every time you hear the Word of God whether you understand it or not. This is the magnificence of the Word. It gives birth to faith when it is sown in your heart and it happens every time you hear the Word of the Kingdom.

On one occasion it was my privilege to speak to about 200 of the wealthiest business men in the nation of South Africa. I did not know anything about them until after I had spoken to them. I shared a very simple Gospel message with them. I challenged them to be real men and receive Jesus as their Lord and Savior. I was not allowed to give a typical altar call. However, I did lead them all in the sinner's prayer. I was able to talk with some of these men at the end of the meeting. Eleven of these wealthy men gave their hearts to Jesus. I did not have time to give them much understanding. But the Word of God caused faith to come alive in their hearts. These eleven men were now born-again. They became a part of the kingdoms I have been writing about.

> *The entrance of thy words giveth light; it giveth understanding unto the simple. (Psalm 119:130)*

First comes the light. **If there is no light, there will never be understanding.** Many other Scriptures express this mystery of the kingdom so very well.

> *For thou wilt light my candle: the lord my God will enlighten my darkness. (Psalm 18:28)*

> *The spirit of man is the candle of the lord, searching all the inward parts of his being. (Proverbs 20:27 - KJV21)*

And the light shineth in darkness; and the darkness comprehended it not. There was a man sent from God, whose name was John. The same came for a witness, to bear witness of the Light, that all men through him might believe. He was not that Light, but was sent to bear witness of that Light. That was the true Light, which lighteth every man that cometh into the world. (John 1:5-9)

But if our gospel be hid, it is hid to them that are lost: In whom the god of this world hath blinded the minds of them which believe not, lest the light of the glorious gospel of Christ, who is the image of God, should shine unto them. (2 Corinthians 4:3-4)

For by grace are ye saved through faith; and that not of yourselves: it is the gift of God: (Ephesians 2:8)

Here is one of my favorites from the Old Testament.

The Lord reigneth; let the earth rejoice; let the multitude of isles be glad thereof. Clouds and darkness are round about him: righteousness and judgment are the habitation of his throne. A fire goeth before him, and burneth up his enemies round about. His lightnings enlightened the world: the earth saw, and trembled. The hills melted like wax at the presence of the Lord, at the presence of the Lord of the whole earth. The Heavens declare his righteousness, and all the people see his glory. (Psalm 97:1-6)

Many people have a lot of the Word in their hearts which they do not understand. Because they have no understanding of what is in their hearts, they never do anything with it. **Understanding only happens when the Word sown in your heart is joined together in your mind.** Paul called this the renewing of the mind.

And be not conformed to this world: but be ye transformed by the renewing of your mind, that ye may prove what is that good, and acceptable, and perfect, will of God. (Romans 12:2)

The person who is renewing their mind is the person with the understanding heart. Renewing your mind is revolutionary. It will change your life. **Renewing your mind will increase the level of understanding in your heart.**

You can receive the benefits of your faith without understanding what is happening to you. However, you usually can't repeat it because you don't understand what happened. A good example of this is what often occurs when new Christians readily receive from God. Then the longer they are saved the less they seem to receive. Their understanding has not increased. Our father does not want us to stay at this level. The Father wants us to move up to higher levels in Him.

Understanding is the link between being a hearer and a doer of the Word. In many cases it has been **the missing link**. Most often, people are not inclined to just go out and do what they hear of the Word.

If this was all it took, the world would be filled with doers of the Word.

Jesus spelled out three levels of understanding in this parable. For some it is an hundredfold, for some sixty, for others it is thirty. **What makes the difference is the level of understanding.**

When Jesus first appeared to the disciples after the resurrection they did not know Him. They did not even believe it was Him.

> *And while they yet believed not for joy, and wondered, he said unto them, have ye here any meat? (Luke 24:41)*

These people had followed Jesus for three years. They heard the Word many times. He told them He must die and would rise from the dead. He was standing right in front of them. They were filled with joy and wonder. They just couldn't seem to believe it was Him. So, Jesus did something to move them into the realm of understanding it was really Him. **He ate something.**

> *And they gave him a piece of a broiled fish, and of an honeycomb. And he took it, and did eat before them. And he said unto them, These are the words which I spake unto you, while I was yet with you, that all things must be fulfilled, which were written in the law of Moses, and in the prophets, and in the psalms, concerning me. Then opened he their understanding, that they might understand the scriptures, And said unto them, Thus it is written, and thus it behooved Christ to suffer, and to rise from the dead the third day: And that repentance and remission of sins should be preached in his name among all nations, beginning at Jerusalem. And ye are witnesses of these things. And, behold, I send the promise of my Father upon you: but tarry ye in the city of Jerusalem, until ye be endued with power from on high. And he led them out as far as to Bethany, and he lifted up his hands, and blessed them. And it came to pass, while he blessed them, he was parted from them, and carried up into Heaven. And they worshiped him,*

> *and returned to Jerusalem with great joy: And*
> *were continually in the temple, praising and*
> *blessing God. Amen. (Luke 24:42-53)*

These are the same people Jesus sent out earlier and told them to heal the sick, cast out devils and raise the dead. They went out and did it, because they believed. They put their faith to work. However, on this day, they took another giant step. He opened their understanding. **Now they had comprehension.**

They followed Jesus to the cross because they believed.

They went to the upper room to wait for the outpouring of the Holy Ghost because they had understanding of God's plan. Now they understood what this was all about. They had a real revelation of Jesus that day. He was no longer just a great man. Jesus was the risen Son of God!

Renewing the mind is the key to understanding. Understanding is the key to revelation. Revelation is essential to knowing the will of God for our lives.

Chapter Fourteen

The Fruit of the Kingdom

———

But he that received seed into the good ground is he that heareth the word, and understandeth it; which also beareth fruit, and bringeth forth, some an hundredfold, some sixty, some thirty. (Matthew 13:23)

I have written about the Word of the Kingdom. I have talked about the mysteries of the kingdom. One of the things I have yet to talk about regarding this parable is **the fruit of the Kingdom.** What is this fruit and how does it grow? How can you tell it is growing? What should we do to help this fruit grow? These are important questions we need to answer.

Obviously, Jesus expects us to bear fruit. So, what is the connection between hearing the Word, understanding the Word and bearing fruit?

As it is described in the parable of the sower the hundred fold return comes in the form of fruit. Jesus spoke about planting **seed**. His focus was on the **soil**. Then as He began explaining the good ground He began talking about **fruit**. This was a common topic for Jesus. But what is this fruit Jesus was talking about in Matthew 13?

It must be the fruit of the spirit.

Jesus gave us great insight into this, which is recorded in the Gospel of John.

> *I am the true vine, and my Father is the husbandman. Every branch in me that beareth not fruit he taketh away: and every branch that beareth fruit, he purgeth it, that it may bring forth more fruit. Now ye are clean through the word which I have spoken unto you. Abide in me, and I in you. As the branch cannot bear fruit of itself, except it abide in the vine; no more can ye, except ye abide in me. I am the vine, ye are the branches: He that abideth in me, and I in him, the same bringeth forth much fruit: for without me ye can do nothing. If a man abide not in me, he is cast forth as a branch, and is withered; and men gather them, and cast them into the fire, and they are burned. If ye abide in me, and my words abide in you, ye shall ask what ye*

will, and it shall be done unto you. Herein is my Father glorified, that ye bear much fruit; so shall ye be my disciples. As the Father hath loved me, so have I loved you: continue ye in my love. If ye keep my commandments, ye shall abide in my love; even as I have kept my Father's commandments, and abide in his love. These things have I spoken unto you, that my joy might remain in you, and that your joy might be full. This is my commandment, That ye love one another, as I have loved you. Greater love hath no man than this, that a man lay down his life for his friends. Ye are my friends, if ye do whatsoever I command you. Henceforth I call you not servants; for the servant knoweth not what his lord doeth: but I have called you friends; for all things that I have heard of my Father I have made known unto you. Ye have not chosen me, but I have chosen you, and ordained you, that ye should go and bring forth fruit, and that your fruit should remain: that whatsoever ye shall ask of the Father in my name, he may give it you. (John 15:1-16)

The **metaphor has changed** in this description of our relationship with God. We are no longer **soil**; we are **branches** in this passage of Scripture. The similarity is found in the mention of the word **fruit**.

Paul used this same metaphor in his writings.

> *But the fruit of the spirit is love, joy, peace, long-suffering, gentleness, goodness, faith, meekness, temperance: against such there is no law. (Galatians 5:22-23)*

From the list of things in the above passage, which Paul has labeled as fruit we can identify two that Jesus mentioned in this teaching recorded in the book of John. Those are the first two on the list in Galatians 5:22. They are love and joy.

Let's make another connection between what Jesus said in the parable of the sower and what He said in the passage in John's Gospel. In the parable, Jesus said several things about the **Word of the Kingdom**. In this passage He also talks about **His words.**

> *If ye abide in me, and my words abide in you, ye shall ask what ye will, and it shall be done unto you. Herein is my Father glorified, that ye bear much fruit; so shall ye be my disciples. (John 15:7-8)*

This is very different language but it is the same concept. It is all about what we do with His words. In the passage in John the emphasis is on the Word abiding in us. God's Word is to be kept in us. It is to remain in us.

The same thing happens when we have understanding. We retain the things we understand. We easily forget what we don't understand.

From these observations, I draw these conclusions. Hearing the Word of the kingdom brings this fruit into our lives. I like to use the fruit of faith as an example.

So then faith cometh by hearing, and hearing by the word of God. (Romans 10:17)

Several translations change the word faith in Galatians 5:22 to faithfulness. This is one way to translate the Greek word for **faith**[1]. I prefer to stay with the way it is translated in the *King James Version* because it helps me to understand something else. It is exactly the same Greek word in both references, so we are not in error in staying with the word faith.

Now connect these two passages of Scripture together in your thinking. Faith comes by hearing the Word of God. Faith is a fruit of the spirit. **Therefore, the fruit of the spirit comes by hearing the Word of God.** All of the fruit comes in this same way. Let's look at the passage in John chapter 15 once again.

These things have I spoken unto you, that my joy might remain in you, and that your joy might be full. (John 15:11)

Because of the words Jesus spoke to the disciples, joy came to them. This is how we receive all nine of the fruit of the spirit. They come to us by hearing the Word. However, Jesus said these words must abide in us.

What causes the Word to abide in us or to remain in us is understanding. I contend this is true because it is understanding the Word which causes this fruit to grow. Like so many things in life this is one of those things which is easier to observe when it does not happen. I am sure you have met Christians who did not seem to have any of this fruit. Yet, they had been saved for years.

I am talking about people who are **not good examples** of what Jesus was teaching in this chapter in the book of John. In fact, they fit very well into at least one of those first three groups of people in the parable of the sower. Think of it like this.

When the Word of the Kingdom comes, the fruit of the spirit comes. **Therefore, whatever happens to the Word also happens to the fruit.** If the Word is snatched away or the Word only remains for a short time because of offenses or the Word is choked out by the cares of this world; the same thing happens to the fruit.

This explains why the fruit of the spirit seems so lacking in the lives of many people who have been saved for many years.

We must hear the Word of the Kingdom. Then we must understand the Word. What is in our hearts from hearing the Word must become joined to our minds. We must understand or comprehend these things so His Word abides in us and we produce much fruit.

Once we connect the fruit of the spirit to the good soil Jesus spoke about it gives much greater understanding to how the fruit develops at different levels.

The difference is in both the hearing of the Word and the understanding of the Word.

Here is a short recap of what I have been sharing with you. First we make a decision for Jesus to be the Lord and Savior of our lives. Then we do whatever it takes to gain understanding of the Word. As our understanding grows we become serious doers of what we now understand. This growing understanding shows up as nine different fruit in our lives which everybody can see and appreciate. The amount of fruit we bear is determined by the level of understanding we have and what we do with what we understand. If we do what we hear, then the fruit grows at a consistent rate. The fruit of the spirit becomes an everyday occurrence in our lives. **The fruit of the spirit defines who we are.**

Chapter Fifteen

Putting the Understanding to Good Use

———

I have one final perspective on the parable of the sower I would like to share with you.

Jesus began the parable talking about a group of people who hear the Word, but they have no understanding of what they hear. This is the **first group** of people, whom Jesus described as *he which received seed by the way side.* But here is the main point I want you to grasp. These people were very religious. Religion has made the Devil's job easy. I am talking about the Christian Religion. It is not supposed to be a religion, but for many this is what it has become. **Religion robs people of the understanding heart.**

This was true in Jesus day. The Jews were expecting the Messiah. For three years He walked among them and stood right in front of them. Yet, what the religious people had taught them about the Messiah was wrong. Many of them did not recognize Jesus for who He was. To this day, they still don't know. This is the tragedy of not understanding the Word. It is easy to take the Word away from people who have no understanding.

Now here is an interesting thought for you.

The Devil knew there would be people who would understand the Word. The people **who did understand** would just keep giving other people the Word of the Kingdom, no matter what. No matter how much they suffered or how many of them the Devil robbed, they would not stop. The Devil needed a plan to defeat this **second group** of people.

The Devil decided to **put rocks in the dirt**. These rocks come in the form of **offenses**. Getting people offended will ruin the dirt. The Word can't take root and grow, at least not for very long. You will not grow spiritually as long as you are offended.

This **second group** starts out with a lot of joy. This is exciting to watch. But getting offended will rob you of the joy. It also opens the door for the wicked one to steal the Word from your heart.

I think there are ministers who confuse people having joy when they hear the Word with people having a sufficient depth of spiritual maturity. These are not the same thing. **Joy does not produce roots.** Understanding produces roots. Jesus said this person has no root in himself.

Joy is only one fruit of the spirit and only one spiritual fruit is not indicative of strong roots.

Just because people enjoy a sermon, or think it is fun to listen to something that makes them laugh, does not mean they are growing spiritually. They may have a good time at church but it does not mean they are growing like they should. **The real test is how they respond under persecution or tribulation.** Do they still have their joy, or do they get offended?

Having joy is not the same as having understanding. If it was, these people would be producing fruit instead of being offended.

The Devil knew if he did not do something to stop these people who were receiving the Word with joy, they would keep hearing the Word until they did understand it. The joy alone would motivate them.

The **third group** of people in the parable of the sower is comprised of those individuals who got caught among the **thorns**. The cares of this life overwhelmed them. The deceitfulness of riches took control of their lives. They only had understanding of the Word for a while.

I can think of no greater example of this than what has happened in the past sixty years in the United States. Many churches experienced phenomenal growth. The response from some of these churches was to take on enormous debt to build larger and grander buildings. The assumption was that this would draw even more people. It did not work. What did happen is a lot of these ministers got caught in the cares of this world due to this burden of debt. Some of them went to Heaven early because of the burden on them. We are not meant to live our lives with the weight of the world on our shoulders.

It has also been sad to watch as ministers, who at one time had been powerful influences in the Kingdom of God got caught in the deceitfulness of riches. In more than one case, it destroyed their ministries. It also ruined marriages and devastated families.

Attempting great things for the Kingdom of God is admirable. I also know this requires great faith. But sometimes what is said to be faith, is not faith at all. It is only a self-centered desire to have more things. Or perhaps it is a craving to be recognized by more of our peers. Often this is what lies behind the decisions which lead a person right into the path of the thorns.

Faith is a fruit of the spirit. Like every other fruit of the spirit, faith must grow. The real purpose for all of the fruit of the spirit is to bring changes into our lives. These changes are intended to make us more like our creator. We should be a reflection of the one who gave us life.

It is the lack of this fruit growing in the lives of many people which has opened the door for the wicked one to get them caught up in the cares of this world and the deceitfulness of riches. Remember, as I have stated previously, fruit is indicative of healthy roots. These healthy roots are a clear sign the Word of the Kingdom has found its place in a person's heart.

When we attempt to receive the benefit of spiritual things which have not developed from an understanding heart, this is a huge mistake. The outward appearance may look very good for a while. However, the real truth eventually is exposed. It is very much like the blackberries no longer being on the vine. All that is left is the thorns.

The **fourth group** of people in the parable, exhibit one of three different levels of understanding. Some understand thirty percent of what they hear. Some understand sixty percent of what they hear. Some understand one hundred percent of what they hear.

My heart's desire is to have one hundred percent understanding and produce one hundred-fold results. To do this means I must understand things I have never heard explained. I must also do things no man has ever taught me to do.

For example, one Sunday in my church I was asked to pray for a man who was scheduled to have surgery on his eye that particular week. I stood in front of this man knowing I was scheduled to have a cataract removed from one of my eyes the very same week. I was aware this man I was about to pray for knew I was going to have surgery on my eye.

I did not know this man who came for prayer. I did not ask him what was wrong with his eye.

Often, I don't ask. **For me to know the problem when I pray for the sick is not a part of the solution.** I just laid my hands on him and commanded his eye to be well.

Later I found out he was legally blind. As a result, he had lost his driver's license, and had not driven his car in five years. The man told me a few Sundays later that his eye doctor had told him he did not expect the surgery to help him much at all. He had the surgery anyway.

After the surgery was done, the man had to wait a few weeks and then go back to the eye doctor to find out the results. He knew he could now see. He just did not know how well until the eye appointment after the surgery and the doctor told him he now has 20/20 vision in his eye. His doctor was surprised at the results.

Does this make sense to you? When you are having a

physical battle with something it can cause questions in your mind about laying hands on another person with a similar problem? How can I expect this man's eye to be healed when I have not received healing for my own eyes? Is it right for me to be laying hands on him so he can receive his healing when I also need healing?

This is what I mean by a **deeper understanding**. I am illustrating for you the **levels of fruit** Jesus spoke of which relate to the **levels of understanding**.

Some think we should not say things like this. It might cause people to question the anointing on us. It might lower other people's opinion of us. That might be a good thing for our ego!

It might bring greater understanding!

I believe any person who is as honest with themselves as they should be has had questions like this. I have never heard them addressed, by anyone at any time. For the most part these questions have been ignored, as though everyone should know the answer. This has robbed us of moving to the highest level of understanding and the highest level of results. Honesty about these matters will free more people to lay hands on the sick.

One thing is certain. If the only people who can pray for the sick are those who never have a physical problem then there will not be anybody praying for the sick. If we cannot lay hands on people and believe God to do things for them which we have not received ourselves then we have a huge problem.

A lack of understanding regarding what I have just shared is the reason many preachers have quit laying hands on the sick. I know this to be a fact because several have admitted this to me.

It almost seems too simple for this to need to be said, but apparently it isn't. Healing will not come to you when I lay my hands on you because of what is going on in my body. Also, you will not fail to receive your healing because I have not received my healing. You will be healed because the spirit of God in me quickens my spirit and delivers healing to you.

> It is the spirit that quickeneth; the flesh prof-
> iteth nothing: the words that I speak unto you,
> they are spirit, and they are life. (John 6:63)

What matters is the words God has given to us.

> So shall my word be that goeth forth out of my
> mouth: it shall not return unto me void, but
> it shall accomplish that which I please, and
> it shall prosper in the thing whereto I sent it.
> (Isaiah 55:11)

The Word is what accomplishes things; not my flesh and not your flesh.

> *My son, attend to my words; incline thine ear unto my sayings. Let them not depart from thine eyes; keep them in the midst of thine heart. For they are life unto those that find them, and health to all their flesh. Keep thy heart with all diligence; for out of it are the issues of life. (Proverbs 4:20-23)*

God's Word, the Word of the Kingdom is health to my flesh. This is one of the secrets of the Kingdom. This is exactly why Jesus refused to speak certain words to the crowds who gathered around Him.

- I refuse to accept the notion: we can't understand why we don't get more people healed. We can and we must understand.
- I refuse to accept the notion: it is just a sovereign act of God when miracles happen. God has made His will very clear. What is our will in the matter?
- I refuse to accept the notion: we have nothing to do with the next Great Awakening. We have everything to do with it. God is waiting on us.

If we are not supposed to understand the things, I have spoken about in this book then why did God tell us to get understanding?

Get wisdom, get understanding: forget it not; neither decline from the words of my mouth. Forsake her not, and she shall preserve thee: love her, and she shall keep thee. Wisdom is the principal thing; therefore get wisdom: and with all thy getting get understanding. (Proverbs 4:5-7)

It is past time for understanding hearts.

When the disciples asked Jesus to explain why he was speaking in parables Jesus said: *"Because it is given unto you to know the mysteries of the Kingdom of Heaven, but to them it is not given." (Matthew 13:11)*

Everything we do not understand is a mystery, or a secret. Once we understand, it is no longer a mystery. We know how to respond. We know how to react. We know who to stay away from and who to move closer to.

It is time to **know** the mysteries of the kingdom.

The Apostle Paul, a man whom I greatly admire, both for his intelligence and his revelation gave us this insight. As you read it, keep in mind Paul is talking about himself.

Though I might also have confidence in the flesh. If any other man thinketh that he hath whereof he might trust in the flesh, I more: And be found in him, not having mine own righteousness, which is of the law, but that which is through the faith of Christ, the righteousness which is of God by faith: That I may know him, and the power of his resurrection, and the fellowship of his sufferings, being made conformable unto his death; If by any means I might attain unto the resurrection of the dead. Not as though I had already attained, either were already perfect: but I follow after, if that I may apprehend that for which also I am apprehended of Christ Jesus. (Philippians 3:4-12)

I still remember reading this one day in my dorm room when I was a student in Bible school. What struck me very forcibly was these words from Paul, *"That I may know him."* I remember thinking at the time, if Paul does not know Him, how could I possibly know Him? It was in fact these very thoughts which caused me to begin searching for a deeper understanding of the rest of this passage of scripture.

The Greek word translated **attained**[1] means - to receive what is given - to experience. The Greek word translated **apprehend**[2] means - to lay hold of - to understand.

Here are the next two verses in this wonderful passage.

Brethren, I count not myself to have apprehended: but this one thing I do, forgetting those things which are behind, and reaching forth unto those things which are before, I press toward the mark for the prize of the high calling of God in Christ Jesus.
(Philippians 3:13-14)

Using the definitions of the words **attained** and **apprehend** which I just shared, I will restate Paul's remarks beginning with verse 12.

Not as though I had already attained (I certainly have not done so. I have not received every healing and victory over every disease. Neither have I experienced everything Jesus provided. I definitely am not perfect,) but I follow after, if that I may (lay hold of and understand) that for which also I am laid hold of by Christ Jesus. Brethren, I count not myself to have apprehended: (I don't have it all yet and I don't understand it all yet:) but this one thing I do, forgetting those things which are behind, and reaching forth unto those things which are before, (I choose not to allow the past to control what I do today. My focus is on what lies out ahead of me.) I press toward the mark for the prize of the high calling of God in Christ Jesus. (Philippians 3:4-16 author's paraphrase)

What is this mark which Paul mentioned?

The mark is the goal of having a one hundred fold

understanding of the Word of the Kingdom. This is our goalpost. I realize some might say this can't be achieved. I believe it can. Otherwise, why did Jesus say these things in His teaching? I do not mean by my statements that we can or will have full understanding of absolutely everything in the Bible. But I do feel the necessity of these questions. Why not try to understand the part we do know? Why not increase our level of understanding of the things we have heard?

What is the prize? It begins with doing the works Jesus did. My, what a prize this would be! What if all the people in one church service were healed? Why stop at one service? Why not expect this in every service? What if all the sinners in church services around the world received Jesus as their Lord? I can't think of a better prize. This is why I was apprehended.

What is the prize? The prize is revelation knowledge. It is receiving truth I did not know before and could not know by myself.

What is the prize? Ultimately, the prize is results!

I will not wait until I have all revelation or understand it all. I will act on what I know now. If you will do the same your understanding heart will increase. You can live the rest of your life with an understanding heart. And most of all, we will have been pleasing to God.

Notes

Chapter 2

1. "H3045 - yada` - Strong's Hebrew Lexicon (KJV)." Blue Letter Bible. Accessed 22 Apr, 2020. https://www.blueletterbible.org//lang/Lexicon/Lexicon.cfm?Strongs=H3045&t=KJV

2. "H2451 - chokmah - Strong's Hebrew Lexicon (KJV)." Blue Letter Bible. Accessed 22 Apr, 2020. https://www.blueletterbible.org//lang/Lexicon/Lexicon.cfm?Strongs=H2451&t=KJV

3. "H998 - biynah - Strong's Hebrew Lexicon (KJV)." Blue Letter Bible. Accessed 22 Apr, 2020. https://www.blueletterbible.org//lang/Lexicon/Lexicon.cfm?Strongs=H998&t=KJV

Chapter 6

1. "G5133 - trapezitēs - Strong's Greek Lexicon (KJV)." Blue Letter Bible. Accessed 22 Apr, 2020. https://www.blueletterbible.org//lang/Lexicon/Lexicon.cfm?Strongs=G5133&t=KJV

2. "G5110 - tokos - Strong's Greek Lexicon (KJV)." Blue Letter Bible. Accessed 22 Apr, 2020. https://www.blueletterbible.org//lang/Lexicon/Lexicon.cfm?Strongs=G5110&t=KJV

Chapter 7

1. "G602 - apokalypsis - Strong's Greek Lexicon (KJV)." Blue Letter Bible. Accessed 22 Apr, 2020. https://www.blueletterbible.org//lang/Lexicon/Lexicon.cfm?Strongs=G602&t=KJV

2. "G3975 - pachynō - Strong's Greek Lexicon (KJV)." Blue Letter Bible. Accessed 22 Apr, 2020. https://www.blueletterbible.org//lang/Lexicon/Lexicon.cfm?Strongs=G3975&t=KJV

3. Google Dictionary

Chapter 8

1. "G4920 - syniēmi - Strong's Greek Lexicon (KJV)." Blue Letter Bible. Accessed 22 Apr, 2020. https://www.blueletterbible.org//lang/Lexicon/Lexicon.cfm?Strongs=G4920&t=KJV

2. "G726 - harpazō - Strong's Greek Lexicon (KJV)." Blue Letter Bible. Accessed 22 Apr, 2020. https://www.blueletterbible.org//lang/Lexicon/Lexicon.cfm?Strongs=G726&t=KJV

Chapter 10

1. "G3718 - orthotomeō - Strong's Greek Lexicon (KJV)." Blue Letter Bible. Accessed 23 Apr, 2020. https://www.blueletterbible.org//lang/Lexicon/Lexicon.cfm?Strongs=G3718&t=KJV

Chapter 11

1. "G1097 - ginōskō - Strong's Greek Lexicon (KJV)." Blue Letter Bible. Accessed 24 Apr, 2020. https://www.blueletterbible.org//lang/Lexicon/Lexicon.cfm?Strongs=G1097&t=KJV

Chapter 12

1. "H7225 - re'shiyth - Strong's Hebrew Lexicon (KJV)." Blue Letter Bible. Accessed 24 Apr, 2020. https://www.blueletterbible.org//lang/Lexicon/Lexicon.cfm?Strongs=H7225&t=KJV

2. "H7341 - rochab - Strong's Hebrew Lexicon (KJV)." Blue Letter Bible. Accessed 24 Apr, 2020. https://www.blueletterbible.org//lang/Lexicon/Lexicon.cfm?Strongs=H7341&t=KJV

3. "H3820 - leb - Strong's Hebrew Lexicon (KJV)." Blue Letter Bible. Accessed 24 Apr, 2020. https://www.blueletterbible.org//lang/Lexicon/Lexicon.cfm?Strongs=H3820&t=KJV

4. "G1994 - epistrephō - Strong's Greek Lexicon (KJV)." Blue Letter Bible. Accessed 24 Apr, 2020. https://www.blueletterbible.org//lang/Lexicon/Lexicon.cfm?Strongs=G1994&t=KJV

5. "G1994 - epistrephō - Strong's Greek Lexicon (KJV)." Blue Letter Bible. Accessed 24 Apr, 2020. https://www.blueletterbible.org//lang/Lexicon/Lexicon.cfm?Strongs=G1994&t=KJV

Chapter 13

1. "G4920 - syniēmi - Strong's Greek Lexicon (KJV)." Blue Letter Bible. Accessed 24 Apr, 2020. https://www.blueletterbible.org//lang/Lexicon/Lexicon.cfm?Strongs=G4920&t=KJV

Chapter 14

1. "G4102 - pistis - Strong's Greek Lexicon (KJV)." Blue Letter Bible. Accessed 24 Apr, 2020. https://www.blueletterbible.org//lang/Lexicon/Lexicon.cfm?Strongs=G4102&t=KJV

Chapter 15

1. "G2983 - lambanō - Strong's Greek Lexicon (KJV)." Blue Letter Bible. Accessed 24 Apr, 2020. https://www.blueletterbible.org//lang/Lexicon/Lexicon.cfm?Strongs=G2983&t=KJV

2. "G2638 - katalambanō - Strong's Greek Lexicon (KJV)." Blue Letter Bible. Accessed 24 Apr, 2020. https://www.blueletterbible.org//lang/Lexicon/Lexicon.cfm?Strongs=G2638&t=KJV